No Quota!

The Speeder's Bible

*Excuses, Smoke Screens, &
Justifications to Use when
Stopped by the Police*

MARCUS MANN

Featuring the International
***Donut Rating System*®**
To Maximize Safe & Immediate Use

DEDICATIONS

Dedicated to the victims, young and old, forever impacted by the reckless disregard of drunken drivers, untreated alcoholics, and addicts unable to find the real solution. A portion of the proceeds from this publication will go directly to nonprofit victim and treatment services.

And to my mother, a real modern day hero: *Florence May Johnson*, who always found the humor in everything! Her contagious laugh has always been the most powerful medicine for all. I thank her for laughing out loud and sometimes just laughing out of courtesy.

THANKS MOM!

And to my mentor, *Sergio*, who insisted on accountability, responsibility, and an honest effort in balancing the books on mistakes of the past.

THANKS SERGIO!

BASED ON ACTUAL STATEMENTS
MADE BY MOTOR VEHICLE DRIVERS
(AND THOSE ATTEMPTING TO DRIVE)
WHEN CONTACTED BY THE POLICE.

LEGAL DISCLAIMER #1:

THE NAMES AND ADDRESSES OF ALL VIOLATORS HAVE BEEN CHANGED TO PROTECT THE INNOCENT, AVOID EMBARASSMENT, SHAME, AND ANY NEGATIVE IMPACT TO THE REAL ESTATE PRICES IN THEIR NEIGBORHOODS.

LEGAL DISCLAIMER #2:

THE USE OF OUR PATENTED **DONUT RATING SYSTEM**® OUTLINED IN THIS BOOK IS NOT INTENDED TO DISPARAGE, DISCREDIT, DAMAGE, EXPOSE, NEGATIVELY IMPACT, OR INFLUENCE THE MARKET OF ANY PASTRY, FRITTER, CAKE DONUT OR MAPLE BAR. DISCLAIMER INCLUDES JELLY-FILLED, POWDERED, OR PLAIN DONUTS. ANY NAME, DESCRIPTION OR SIMILARITY TO AN ACTUAL DONUT IS PURELY COINCIDENTAL.

PASTRY RIGHTS DISCLAIMER:

LIVE DONUTS WERE NOT USED DURING ANY PORTION OF THIS PUBLICATION - PRE OR POST PRODUCTION. WE DO NOT CONDONE THE MISTREATMENT OF DONUTS.

INTRODUCTION

No Quota – The Speeders Bible, follows the theme of my first helpful manual, *I had to Drive, I was too Drunk to Walk;* however, I've added volumes of material related to the decision making process of the Police Officer. You should find the tips helpful as you consider how to cajole and guide (or manipulate) the officer who is about to dictate your future insurance rates and sometimes your freedom. This text includes a cheerful look at a serious topic – poor driving, tragic circumstances, and comical comments. It includes a few of my old favorites and a ton of new material and meaningful editorial. I've assembled the pages from police traffic stops, accident scenes, and during those Driving Under the Influence (DUI) arrests. Some quips are from my individual experience as a Peace Officer and others were shared by contemporaries from across the country. **No Quota** is a compilation of the smartest words and some of the most pitiful smoke screens heard during the regressive slide into childlike fear after one is stopped by the police.

With keen attention to each excuse, you'll learn what's hot and what's not in the mind of the police as they process our sometimes wild excuses. *If you have a pulse,* you will be entertained while also gaining great insight as you throw your head back and laugh through the pages. I find it glorious how the pressure of blue lights, a badge, a dose of ego, and lots of leather, frighten us into bizarre, twisted and wordy lies. I've prepared a healthy rating system to aid you in deciding what smoke screen or quality excuse may work best for you:

Each excuse or justification in this book is accompanied by a risk rating:

1. Low Risk = Five Donuts:

A Fantastic Excuse to Use on *THE MAN*
(slang for police)

2. Moderate Risk = Three Donuts:

A So-So Excuse to Use on 5-0
(also slang for police)

3. High Risk = One Donut:

Your Excuse Sucks
& You're at Risk

4. No Donut, Step Out of the Car:

You Probably Blew It!
Good Luck!

In addition to the rating system, I've added an editorial that includes what the **_driver said_** to the officer followed by what the **_officer heard_** - or how the driver's words were interpreted. This point of view is an exclusive look, providing you with the unique peek at the mental processes behind the decision to write a ticket, arrest the driver, or give a verbal warning. Here's an example:

- **What the driver said:** *"I did nothing wrong, officer. I can't believe you guys are always harassing me! I want your name and badge number!"*

- **What the officer heard:** *"Uh oh! I'm another do-gooder who thinks the world is wrong and I am always right. Yes, I said 'always harassing me' as I'm not only a do-gooder ... I've also been stopped by the police quite often and can't learn my lesson. I think you can help me in two areas: Give me your name – just like I demanded – in the signature block on multiple tickets."*

Please keep in mind, my humor, mockery and editorial comments are meant to be good-natured advice – offering an inside look at the mysterious thought process of the officer. Please share these tips with your family and friends, especially the speed demon on Testosterone. Remember: If stopped by **_The Man_**, carefully choose only one excuse, give it an Academy Award delivery, and hope the officer has not heard it before. This will keep you and your mouth in *low-donut territory*.

More on Driver Risk & Ratings:

When the police stop you all justifications leaking from your mouth carry risk. A driver may use a first-class excuse and get a ticket anyway. Conversely, a driver may use a total flop and end up with no citation whatsoever. Why? The complexity is in the many factors influencing the adrenaline driven thought process called "*officer discretion*".

Bear in mind, contrary to some accounts, police officers (also called *5-0, The Heat, One-Time, Po-po, and The Man),* are human beings. Humans are biased by memories, experience, and upbringing. So, select your looks carefully and pay keen attention to your demeanor, car style, clothing, cologne, sports team, your car freshener, bumper stickers, your wheels, the lighting, your loud music, and the tint of your windows. No pressure, but, yes, **the officer is profiling you**. He is also profiling everything around you; the studded dog collar on your neck, decorations stapled to your face, lips, and eyebrows, low riding jeans, and the Anarchist tattoo on your left forearm! The police – and therefore YOU - have many variables to consider. Most importantly, the officer is profiling every word as it flows from the pie hole – politely called your mouth!

Beyond countless cosmetic factors, the most critical moment of interaction with the officer is - and always will be - when you open your mouth! Your words will often determine the outcome of the traffic stop. Regardless of color, creed, sexual orientation, religion, age, or multiple piercings – your mouth is the deciding factor. **The Man** does not care what color you are or if you're male, female, bi-transferable, transgendered, a transformer, or just not sure. He's trying determine if you are honest, need a ticket or a verbal warning.

So, dress nice, keep all your body parts covered, and don't blow it when you open your mouth.

As I mentioned earlier, each excuse is accompanied by the risk rating: *Five Donuts, Three Donuts, One Donut*, and *No Donut, Step Out of the Car.* The risk rating aligns with the probability of arrest or citation when you use this style of excuse. *Five Donut* excuses are the best and may be used fresh out of the box. If the excuse is followed by the rating *No Donut, Step Out of the Car*, DON"T USE IT! Use of this excuse or justification normally guarantees you will be booked into jail.

Since my first book, ***I had to Drive, I was Too Drunk to Walk***, I've heard from some of you. Some bragged about how well the low-risk excuses worked for them when stopped for speeding. Others wrote to curiously state how mad they were after they used an excuse or a joke that was clearly identified as high risk. Let me say it again: *Donuts Good - No Donuts Bad!* If the excuse has no donuts in the risk rating, don't use it!

Got it? Good! Let's have some fun!

EXCUSE NUMBER 1

When stopped for speeding, the driver stated,

"Dude, what is your immediate crisis?"

Risk Rating: Careful! High Risk - One Donut

Your Excuse Sucks & You're at Risk

You will likely see the officer crack a mild, relaxed smile immediately after these words catch air. Not because he is happy - he's smiling because you just helped him save time in his decision making process. Yep, you are getting a ticket.

This brusque statement is *no way* to start a short-term relationship with a cop. *"What's your problem"* or *"What is your Crisis,"* infers the officer has the problem instead of you. Remember, police officers don't stop someone because they're looking for a critic.   They're simply doing their job and that happens to be you!

- **What the driver said:** *"Dude, what is your immediate crisis?"*

- **What the officer heard:** *"I'm an elite member of the community, I make no mistakes, and I will never learn anything without losing some money.*

  I really want a ticket because I hate authority and always try to push blame onto my kids, my wife, my boss, and my girlfriend – the sister of my wife. I have no humility, and I'm never wrong, and I need discipline. I not only need a citation, I would love three tickets."

- **Final thought:** *Dude, pull your head out of the darkness!*

EXCUSE NUMBER 2

When stopped for speeding, the driver stated,

**"I'm off to the hospital. My girlfriend is an
Emergency Room nurse and my wife
is getting stitches."**

Risk Rating: Moderate Risk - Three Donuts

A So-So Excuse to Use on 5-0

Yuk! It sounds like this driver is cooking up some dysfunctional stew. This excuse is an unwise attempt at the truth. It's pretty obvious that the driver is stressed and has a very good reason to be maxed out. Officers love the truth and nobody can tell a lie that sounds this harebrained.

Attempts at openness are always appreciated. And, if this was my situation, I'd probably get stopped for speeding too - during my race to get out of town! This is a three donut excuse because of the honesty of the driver and because the officer may take pity on the guy.

- **What the driver said:** *"I'm off to the hospital. My girlfriend is an Emergency Room nurse and my wife is getting stitches."*

- **What the officer heard:** *"I'm off to the hospital to continue my quest of creating an absolute mess in the lives of three people.*

Yes, it appears that accountability has reared its ugly head and Karma is standing by the hospital to welcome me. Officer, a ticket is deserved; however, my destiny will soon be complete, and I'll be dead in about thirty minutes and unable to pay the fine."

- **Final thought:** *In some cases, the officer may follow the driver to the hospital. Not for anything other than pure entertainment. A little cold but true.*

EXCUSE NUMBER 3

A drunk driver, after being stopped, accidently put his car into reverse and rammed the police car behind him, he stated,

"Geez Officer ...that was stupid. Don't you know how to drive?"

Risk Rating: No Donut - Step out of the car!

You Probably Blew It! Good Luck!

Driver, you are lucky you didn't get shot and that the officer was able to jump out of the way. Come on! I don't know of any officer who accidently puts his patrol car in "Drive" and rams a drunk. This comment is incredible and the driver was honored by an immediate arrest and booking. He earned a trip to the slammer and a couple of additional charges.

Typically, once the officer knows you're drunk, she will make the arrest right away. In this case, ramming the police car was a clue. The driver removed all reasonable doubt when he opened his mouth and tried to blame the officer.

- **What the driver said:** *"Geez Officer... that was stupid. Don't you know how to drive?"*

- **What the officer heard:** *"I'm drunk and a little crazy. I'm drunk enough to hit a police vehicle*

*and conditioned enough (on alcohol) to blame
you for it. I also blame my boss, my wife, my
kids, and the government for all my ills. I
need some humility and accountability ... I
need to be booked."*

- **Final thought:** *This happened at 6:30 in the
evening. Your thoughts?*

EXCUSE NUMBER 4

When stopped for speeding and asked, "Do you know how fast you were going?" the driver stated,

"Dude! I can't keep my eyes on the road and text at the same time."

Risk Rating: Careful! High Risk - One Donut

Your Excuse Sucks & You're at Risk

Surly and derisive comments like this may work well in his short-term marriage, but they're not recommended for a police officer. If you want to be cute when you're stopped by one of us, be sure you have an extra five hundred bucks to blow. If you want to blow a lot of money, say something like "dude." Generally, if we stop someone for speeding, they were probably speeding! This guy added the "texting" element to the equation, which nearly guarantees a ticket.

- **What the driver said:** *"Dude! I can't keep my eyes on the road and text at the same time."*

- **What the officer heard:** *"I'm calling you dude for a reason. I smoke lots of weed in between skateboarding parks and I rarely drive because I'm only 32 and my mom won't lone me the car. In fact, I'm likely under the influence of some bad assed, BC Bud as we speak. I'm texting my boarder-friend to score more smoke. Did I say dude? What I meant to say was I have no respect for authority and* *have a tattoo on my calf of a pot bellied pig wearing a police hat. Dude, please search my car."*

- **Final thought:** *Officers do not like to be called Dude, Bitch, Honey-pie, Punk, Miss Piggy, Bacon, or late for dinner. Stay safe, stay professional, and keep it formal.*

EXCUSE NUMBER 5

When stopped for speeding (75 in a 55 MPH zone), weaving all over the road with no windshield in his truck, the 45 year old country boy driver said,

"Sorry Officer, I seem to have something in my eye."

Risk Rating: High Risk - One Donut

Your Excuse Sucks & You're at Risk

Oh my! This is pitiful and funny. *Hmm, how did I get this bug in my eye?* This guy earned a *"High-Risk"* rating for two reasons: 1) He's dangerous to other drivers and, 2) He's dangerous to himself. In driving over the speed limit without a windshield, the driver may be borderline insane.

This driver was actually surprised he had something in his eye – a bug, dirt, a small bird or whatever in the world had imbedded in his face. Wow! One would think he would be driving slowly on the shoulder of the road with hazard flashers. But, *Noooo!* He was driving 20 over the limit. Upon reflection, he seemed to have a bunch of stuff in his teeth too!

- **What the driver said:** *"Sorry Officer, I seem to have something in my eye."*

- **What the officer heard:** *"Howdy Officer, I don't understand the law of cause and effect. I have a very different perspective on life and* *how best to enjoy Mother Nature. In fact, when my wife was pregnant with twins, I was so mad I went out looking for the other guy! I am the perfect candidate for a ticket."*

EXCUSE NUMBER 6

When stopped for speeding, the driver claimed,

"Three guys are chasing me."

Risk Rating: Moderate Risk - Three Donuts

A So-So Excuse to Use on 5-0

Running from others is a bad sign! It is not common and will only work if you can produce the "Three Guys." Not so great when the officer can't find the three guys or whatever you're running from. You can easily bump this excuse into the "*High Risk - One Donut*" category if you don't provide a name or a reason you are being chased.

You can also create a real problem for yourself if you say "*Some black guys are chasing me.*" That one is truly overused and not very nice. In any case, if those "guys" are on your tail, look at your lifestyle or move out of our jurisdiction.

- **What the driver said:** *"Three guys are chasing me."*

- **What the officer heard:** *"Officer, I said 'Three' because it is the number I always use when I'm lying. 'Guys are chasing me' is the term I use every time I'm looking around to score some dope and I run into you! I'm just avoiding responsibility for my actions.*

Hmmm... you can't call me a liar so just write me a ticket instead."

- **Final thought:** *If someone is chasing you, drive to a fire station or a police department. Don't make the mistake this guy made and keep driving circles in the area known for street level narcotic sales.*

EXCUSE NUMBER 7

When stopped after running several red lights and speeding, the driver explained,

"I'm 12 weeks pregnant."

Risk Rating: Yes! Five Donuts! - Low Risk!

A Fantastic Excuse to Use on *THE MAN*, unless......

A baby on board works nearly every time! Police are usually lenient when someone needs to get to the hospital and bring a new life into the world. 12 weeks is a tad early – don't you think? And another thing, you'd better be female (or have one aboard), you'd better be pregnant (or have a pregnant passenger), and you'd better be on your way to the hospital.

During the above traffic stop, the risk rating jumped to "*No donut, step out of the car*," when the officer discovered the sole occupant/driver was actually a well-dressed man. True story!

- **What the driver said:** *"I'm 12 weeks pregnant."*

- **What the officer heard:** *"I'm 12 weeks pregnant and have a really big Adams Apple. I'm not only a traffic violator, but double as a liar, a freak, and one who will use a pregnant woman as a shield. I don't deserve a ticket. I* *actually have a primal desire for jail. Lots of vulnerable men in jail right? Remember to tell the jailers to segregate me for two reasons: You don't know if I'm a male or a female and spending time in my own cell is best for me. Please hang the dress in the appropriate fashion baggie."*

- **Final thought:** *We don't give a hoot about sexuality or how you dress. Don't lie and don't use the vulnerable or less fortunate within your excuse unless it is true.*

EXCUSE NUMBER 8

When stopped for suspicion of drunk driving,
the driver stated,

"You can't arrest me, I'm Broke Obama."

Risk Rating: High Risk - One Donut

Your Excuse Sucks & You're at Risk

The officer is now thinking: "*Is this guy cracked or just drunk*?" In either case, this driver must be considered for arrest - taken into custody for his own safety and definitely for society's health. Claiming to be Bush, Elvis Presley, Puff Daddy, the President, or any high-visibility character will often get you a guaranteed free room for the night.

- **What the driver said:** *"You can't arrest me, I'm Broke Obama."*

- **What the officer heard:** *"What I meant to say was 'please arrest me.' Whenever I use the word CAN'T, I actually mean DO IT. Sorry for the misunderstanding. Also, 5-0, I didn't realize you were a Republican when I used my poorly formed false name. Can I change my lie to Nancy Pelosi? Not good? Okay, how about Ted Kennedy? Okay, okay, okay … I'm also politically ignorant about who's dead. Is that another charge?"*

- **Breathalyzer results:** .26

EXCUSE NUMBER 9

When stopped for speeding, 41 in a 25 MPH zone,
the driver stated,

"Officer, think carefully before you write me a ticket."

Risk Rating: High Risk - One Donut

Your Excuse Sucks & You're at Risk

What? I'm not sure I'm picking up what you're putting down, Mr. Driver. Hmm, let's see. Is this a comment? Is it a threat? Is it a strange new game show? Do I win a prize if I *think carefully* before I scratch out a ticket? Just what is the theory behind using such a comment? This type of veiled threat usually pops out of a REALLY important and egocentric bore. Strike that! This type of veiled threat leaks out of someone who THINKS they're important.

After hearing this excuse, an officer will probably respond, *"Considering I don't know who you are, please sign here so I can remember your name."*

- **What the driver said:** *"Officer, think carefully before you write me a ticket."*

- **What the officer heard:** *"Officer, I've abused people and power for ages and ages. I am a legend in my own mind. Yep, I'm a self made man and I worship my maker. My kids and wife are terrified of me, my employees do not like*

*me, and my friends are ego maniacs too!
Officer, the only hope I have is you. Please
calibrate my compass by writing a ticket."*

- **Final thought:** *This is a guaranteed ticket.
The ego-monster might get it dismissed in
court; however, a ticket is very likely.*

EXCUSE NUMBER 10

At the scene of an accident where a car hit a building, the driver stated,

"We were throwing eggs at people and I dropped one on the floor."

Risk Rating: High Risk - One Donut

Your Excuse Sucks & You're at Risk

This driver likely earned a ticket and possibly an arrest, especially if one of the people he threw the eggs at earlier was the same officer on foot patrol. True story - same cop. Pranks are great until they lead to this sort of result! I'd have another question for the driver: *"What does it feel like to have a little egg in your face?"*

- **What the driver said:** *"We were throwing eggs at people and I dropped one on the floor."*

- **What the officer heard:** *"I am the Satan-spawn that threw the yolk-ball at you two hours ago – an act of complete disobedience to God's Law. I prefer no breaks and would greatly appreciate to be loaded with criminal charges of biblical proportion. While you don't know this, you will be saving my future by giving me a criminal charge for every egg launched from my vehicle … thank you officer … may I have another?"*

- **Final thought:** *Hitting an on-duty cop with anything is normally a felony. This includes eggs, snowballs, spitballs, poop balls, etc. I know, "How was I supposed to know that? It felt so natural at the time I did it."*

EXCUSE NUMBER 11

When stopped for speeding (clocked on radar going 84 in a 60 zone), the driver stated,

"This is not my car, his speedometer said 70 and my radar detector never let out a peep."

Risk Rating: High Risk - One Donut

Your Excuse Sucks & You're at Risk

Ah ha! Hot on the scent of a chronic speeder with no accountability. When we stop someone with a radar detector it's like striking gold – akin to finding a cure for cancer or locating a woman who loves to watch pro football. It's, it's like ... hold on, I need a cigarette. It's unbelievably great – tingly, warm, and refreshing. It makes our day when a habitual traffic offender (like this one) is caught.

Do you ever wonder what traffic cops talk about when they go home at night? Tremendous victories like this! The moral of the story is don't brag about a radar detector while saying you don't understand the mechanics of the borrowed car. Keep it out of sight and shut up! Dress up your police detector like a Kleenex box, or baseball hat, or a large bong ... but don't make it so darn easy for us.

- **What the driver said:** *"This is not my car, his speedometer said 70 and my radar detector never peeped."*

- **What the officer heard:** *"I love you so much officer, I'm going to share some words you only dream about: I'm a dork and I'm driving a borrowed car, but I do own my own radar detector and took the time to install it. I drive over the speed limit ALL THE TIME. Please give me the spanking I never received as a child. Only two citations? Oh, come on. Is that all you have in you today … wimp? Atta boy, four tickets should do the trick!"*

- **Final thought:** *Courtesy good – radar detector bad!*

EXCUSE NUMBER 12

When stopped for suspicion of drunk driving,
the drive stated,

"If I tell you a good joke, will you let me go?"

The officer answered, "Well…maybe."

Driver: "What's the difference between a cop
and a cowboy?"

Officer: "I don't know, sir."

Driver: "The cowboy has the crap on the
OUTSIDE of his boots."

Officer: "No Donut - Step out of the Car!"

Risk Rating: ditto

You Blew It! Tell the joke again to your new
cell mate!

Man, what were you thinking? Mildly intoxicated and
telling a breathy joke to a cop? A cop who's not yet
decided what he's going to do? A CRAP JOKE no
less? A pasture manure joke inferring the cop is
CRAP?

Most officers have a fantastic sense of humor, but watch the material and the punch line! This set up is akin to telling sex offender jokes in a daycare center. It doesn't even slightly fit the environment. Funny joke and expensive outcome!

- **What the driver said:** *"If I tell you a good joke, will you let me go?"*

- **What the officer heard:** *"I have an impulse control problem and a tendency to do and say really stupid stuff at just the wrong moment. Okay? Here we go ... If my joke sucks I need you to really bust my butt. Oh, so you didn't like the Crap-Cowboy-monologue? Okay, okay, okay, let's try another one ... These two transgendered cops skip into a bar holding hands and singing praises to Rodney King ... and one of the officers is you. Ouch, those cuffs hurt. Geez, you're a sensitive little pork product. Ouch! No so rough!"*

EXCUSE NUMBER 13

When stopped for speeding (clocked on radar going 84 in a 55 MPH zone), the driver stated,

Officer, my car was designed in Europe For the Autobahn. I get better mileage at these speeds."

Risk Rating: High Risk - One Donut

Your Excuse Sucks & You're at Risk

This justification is exceedingly precarious. Here's why: 1) this is not Europe and, 2) this is not the Autobahn. The officer's thought process went something like this: *"Hmm, European sports car. He knows about the German Autobahn and probably travels a lot. He wears those driving gloves with the funky little knuckle holes. He DOESN'T have one of those Christmas tree air fresheners. Yep, he can afford a ticket."*

Remember: The officer is profiling you! Drivers and their cars have a portrait and this guy just bought himself a free driver's profile. What is your profile?

- **What the driver said:** *Officer, my car was designed in Europe for the Autobahn. I get better mileage at these speeds."*

- **What the officer heard:** *"Officer, I have a lot of money and I don't plan on driving your speed limit - ever. Quick, write me while you can."*

EXCUSE NUMBER 14

When stopped for suspicion of drunk driving and speeding, the driver stated,

"I figured I'd spend half the time on the road by driving twice as fast."

Risk Rating: No Donut - Step out of the Car!

You Probably Blew It! Good Luck!

Whoa! This is a very interesting excuse indeed. An operational yet polluted brain behind the wheel. After a couple of beers, this one almost sounds plausible. I should say after a couple of beers, a nibble of Oxycodone, and three big draws from the BC Bud Bong. Well, it didn't work so well in this case.

Some officers may laugh and let you go if you were merely in a parking lot; however, that wasn't the case. Once the officer saw his eyes, took a whiff of the many of illegal fragrances wafting from his orifices, she did laugh - all the way to the booking desk.

- **What the driver said:** *"I figured I'd spend half the time on the road by driving twice as fast."*

- **What the officer heard:** *"Officer, I need to go jail and think about what my zany rationale may have meant and where it came from. A little voice in my head said this was okay to do and* *okay to say. My 'little invisible friend' seems to cause lots of problems for me these days. Once you book me, you can have some quiet time to yourself and try to figure out what in the heck I meant by this excuse."*

EXCUSE NUMBER 15

After pulling up to several red lights, honking twice, and proceeding through the solid red light, the 76 year old man stated,

"I can't stop at these lights anymore. Last time I did some guy rear-ended me."

Risk Rating: Yes! Five Donuts! - Low Risk!

A Fantastic Excuse to Use on *THE MAN*

Oh yea! This excuse has the magical appeal that softens the heart of any traffic cop with a pulse. Nobody and I mean nobody can lie about something like this. His misjudgment is understandable considering his past experiences. Remember, the officer can and did check this man's driving history - a member of our Greatest Generation. He HAD in fact been the victim of a rear end collision. What'd he get? He received a soft-spoken lecture and kind advice on drivers training. Solid excuse! Good job!

- **What the driver said:** *"I can't stop at these lights anymore. Last time I did some guy rear-ended me."*

- **What the officer heard:** *"I can't lie and I'm afraid. I don't know what else to do and I can't physically handle another collision. I fought in*

WWII, survived the depression, and I'm swimming in a world of unethical business and insensitivity. Please have grace on me."

- **Final thought:** *Honesty and honor sells with most Peace Officers.*

EXCUSE NUMBER 16

When stopped for speeding, the driver stated,

"I'll trade you a doughnut for a warning."

Risk Rating: High Risk - One Donut
(or maybe two)

Your Excuse Sucks & You're at Risk

We'd be millionaires if we had a dollar for every *doughnut joke* we've heard. Some pastry humor is actually funny. As most professional comedians say, *"Timing is everything."* I can use donuts in my book because I was a career officer and have earned the right to sell donut humor! Minorities can tell certain jokes, amputees can use self deprecating humor, and those with Alzheimer's ... well, never mind. But when it comes to donut jokes ... cover your ass when stopped by the man.

This driver's timing was way off. The driver got four tickets for a total of $1146.00 dollars. That's a boat load of donuts! Next time, try a lawyer joke, a politician joke, or tell one of those Fatal-Stupid-Crook-Darwin stories. 5-0 likes Darwin stories. Remember: When you're with your defense lawyer, tell cop jokes. When you're with your new friend the officer, tell lawyer jokes. Got it?

- **What the driver said:** *"I'll trade you a doughnut for a warning."*

- **What the officer heard:** *"I'm a smart ass with poop for timing. Not just any smart ass … I'm THE *Smartest Assiest one of the patrol shift and strongly lust after an expensive ticket."*

*Note: The thought process of an officer does not have to be grammatically correct or sensitive to spelling errors. It's a *thought-process* … get over it.

EXCUSE NUMBER 17

When a driver was stopped for improper lane travel, the officer asked him, "You appear to have some alcohol on board, when did you start drinking?" The driver answered,

"Oh, about twenty-four years ago."

Risk Rating: Moderate Risk - Three Donuts

A So-So Excuse to Use on 5-0

What? That's a lot of drinking! This guy gets a little wiggle room for being funny – though he didn't try to crack a funny. Did this driver understand the question? Ah, then it happens … the drama continues: The officer gets a whiff of funky-breath (and maybe a little urine). There it goes … the wiggle room is gone for the night. Actually, most intoxicated drivers misunderstand all the questions:

Officer: *May I have your name?*

Drunk: *Name, my name? You gonna be fair and give me a few minutes to think on that?*

Officer: Sir, *while you're thinking about your name, what is your address?*

Drunk: *Right now? My address right now?*

Officer: *Yes, what is your address right now?*

Drunk: *Well, what address are we at, do you know, right this minute. What's the address here?*

Officer: *WE are not an address … what is your home address?*

Drunk: *I asked a real question. No reason to be a squiggly little piggy-wiggly.*

Officer: *Sir, turn around and place your hands behind your back. … click!*

Sadly, we have met some drivers who have been drinking nonstop for twenty-plus years. We can always tell when they're going to be difficult – as soon as they open their mouths. This guy fit the description of the chronic alcoholic to a "T" … Don't light a match!

- **What the driver said:** *"Oh, about twenty-four years ago."*

- **What the officer heard:** *"Officer, you should call your family and let them know you will be home late. I'm so drunk you need to take me to the hospital, wait for the alcohol to burn off, and process me for my fifth DUI.*

  After booking, you need to decontaminate your patrol car because I pooped, urinated and puked in your back seat and smeared it around with the dedication of a child finger painting. Let the family know you will be home in four to six hours."

EXCUSE NUMBER 18

A Non-English speaking driver, when stopped for speeding and running a red light, stated,

"I just did crap in me pants."

Risk Rating: Yes! Five Donuts! - Low Risk!

A Fantastic Excuse to Use on *THE MAN*

The officer discovered the driver had in fact soiled his chinos due to illness. Why the Low Risk rating? It has to do with biohazards and the officer's ink pen. When officers write a ticket they hand the pen to the driver to sign the ticket who then returns the pen. Needless to say, this officer didn't want to catch the illness nor have her pen handled by a person who did not have his poop together – so to speak. She let him go.

If you want to try this excuse, by all means **go for it.** Get it? **Go for it.** I know, very immature. You're not my Editor ... rise above it poopy-pants.

- **What the driver said:** *"I just did a crap in my pants."*

- **What the officer heard:** *"I'm from an exotic foreign land and I am sick. I come from a land where people die by the millions from diseases with unknown names. I may be lying about being sick; however, your little police nose is not lying. Yes, the illness I have is leaking from* *me. Yes, those are little poop molecules going up your All American nostrils. The world will be a better place if we minimize the amount of DNA escaping from my SMART car during our brief time together. Is a ticket worth a fatal disease? If fact, don't even ask for my license or my passport. I may be the top dog for Al Qaeda, but it isn't worth your time and health just to see a name on my license ... a name you can't even pronounce."*

- **Final thought:** *Run officer, run ... act like you have an emergency call that mandates your immediate attention ... run! Go for it! Oooo, that was a little funny. I like that part...* **go for it.**

EXCUSE NUMBER 19

*When stopped for running a red light and suspicion of
drunk driving, the driver didn't say anything.*

**Silence as the driver lit a cigarette, turned up
the music, and finished a text message**

Risk Rating: No Donut - Step out of the Car!

You Probably Blew It! Good Luck!

You can't imagine what it's like for a police officer to
have a driver that doesn't say a word on a traffic stop.
Of course, there's a childlike temptation to be quiet
when in trouble. But what's up with the cigarette, the
loud music, and the texting? These little distractions
might have worked with your parents or teachers, but
the silent treatment won't work with a police officer.
Pouting, holding one's breath or throwing a temper
tantrum also fails with 5-0. Try an excuse, any excuse,
but never give us the silent treatment.

Now, if we (the police) historically get the silent
treatment in our family home, you're sure to get
arrested. Do you know why you'll get arrested each
and every time you clam up? Well, I'm not telling you.
You can just suffer! Go ahead ... suffer. I'm so done
talking to you. YOU ARE DEAD TO ME.

- **What the driver said:** *Nothing*

- **What the officer heard:** *The sound of her handcuffs being removed from their case on her belt and firmly placed on the driver.*

EXCUSE NUMBER 20

When stopped for speeding and suspicion of drunk driving, the driver stated,

"I thought this was the drunk-driving lane."

Risk Rating: Moderate Risk - Three Donuts

A So-So Excuse to Use on 5-0

If you're not drunk, this is really funny; however, statements such as these are another clue to what's hidden in the subconscious mind of little Uncle Drunkster.

In this case, the driver was in the carpool lane. He thought he was stopped for a lane violation and his statement to the officer was a wee bit off base because of a few too many cocktails. P.S. This excuse was mentioned at his DUI criminal trial. Uncle Drunkster brought several photos to prove he was actually in the carpool lane and not in the drunk-driving lane. What? Yea, I know ... pitiful and bizarre.

- **What the driver said:** *"I thought this was the drunk-driving lane."*

- **What the officer heard:** *"Officer, I'm so F'd up me can't even confess properly. In fact, I illegally drive in the carpool lane sober. I do it so often when I'm sober it only makes sense right now to call it the drunk-pool lane. Oops. I*

*did it again. I meant to call it beer aisle way, I
mean the cocktail trail; I mean the swifter-snifter
lane. Oh, never mind. Do you want to hear a
joke? Do you know the difference between a
cop and a cowboy?"*

- **Final thought:** Blood alcohol count: .26

EXCUSE NUMBER 21

When stopped for slowing down and then running a red light, the driver stated,

"Dude, I'm sorry. I really didn't see you."

Risk Rating: Moderate Risk - Three Donuts

A So-So Excuse to Use on 5-0

"I'm sorry," is the only reason this excuse got three donuts. The rest of the statement was amusing. If you ever tell an officer, "I'm sorry," you have a better chance of driving away ticket-free. If the cop believes you only obey the law when a police officer is around, well...press hard when you sign as we need four copies.

Think about it in a different context. Imagine you are changing the oil in your car late at night. You have that big-O-tub of dirty oil and decide to pour it down the sewer drain. Greenpeace pulls up in their Zodiac boat, 60's flower van, or whatever, and they say *"Hey, dude, what's up with the oil leak?"* You turn to them and say *"I'm sorry, I really didn't see you."*

Just think about it, **dude.** What's next, cheating on your taxes because no one is watching? Wait, ~~strike that, bad example.~~ What's next, it's okay to cheat on your spouse because no one is watching? I'll make you a deal: It's okay to cheat on your spouse if EVERYONE is watching. Does that make sense? Do the right thing when no one is watching! Note: some tax exemptions are allowed.

- **What the driver said:** *"Dude, I'm sorry. I really didn't see you."*

- **What the officer heard:** *"Dude, I do this all the time. I don't live my life to do the right thing – I survive by making sure I never get caught doing wrong. In fact, I drive around looking for bridges that have a warning sign that says 'don't throw debris from the bridge'… just so I can throw debris over the railing. You better write me a ticket now because I've always got my eye out for you and anyone else in authority."*

EXCUSE NUMBER 22

When stopped for speeding (45 in a 30 MPH zone)
the driver stated,

"I'm almost out of antifreeze!"

Risk Rating: High Risk - One Donut

Your Excuse Sucks & You're at Risk

Oh, whatever! This guy (an engineer for a large aircraft company) went on to explain. He qualified his comment with a windy explanation about the wind speeds, cooling systems, and the speed of his car radiator blade versus the forward speed of his vehicle. He concluded the diatribe with a clear rationale that he was in fact speeding to keep his engine cool. The explanation took about four minutes of non-stop verbal vomiting. This was just enough time for the officer to complete the ticket.

Some excuses may be scientifically sound; however, the officer really doesn't give a hoot. Buy some antifreeze, slow down, and save the engineering hype for the office.

- **What the driver said:** *"I'm almost out of antifreeze!"*

- **What the officer heard:** *"I drank the last swig of antifreeze I had left."*

- **Final thought:** *Antifreeze: $3.74 Ticket:*
  $240.00

EXCUSE NUMBER 23

*When stopped for suspicion of drunk driving,
the driver stated,*

"I had to drive, I was too drunk to walk."

Risk Rating: No Donut - Step out of the car!

You Probably Blew It! Good Luck!

This is the one. My all time favorite – the finest, most ridiculous excuse I've ever heard. And, the driver actually believed this rationale. When we hear a jewel like this, we are bound to summon five or six more squad cars and plead with the subject: *"Please, please say it one more time."*

As you can imagine, this never went to trial. It is one of the best confessions I have ever heard. Thank God the officer stopped this one. He had enough liquor in him to open his own bar.

- **What the driver said:** *"I had to drive, I was too drunk to walk."*

- **What the officer heard:** *"I am totally FUBAR drunk; F'd Up Beyond All Recognition.*

- **Final thought:** Blood Alcohol Count, .31. Yowee!

EXCUSE NUMBER 24

When stopped for speeding and running a red light, the driver asked,

"Wazzup, Big Blue?"

Risk Rating: High Risk - One Donut

Your Excuse Sucks & You're at Risk

This is actually a polite version of Excuse Number One, hence the "high" rating. We call these excuses, *"fillers"* – something the violator says to *"fill in time"* until he or she can think of something more intelligent to say. In this case, the *"more intelligent"* part never really happened. Sometimes we even answer this dumb question with statements like:

"Wazzup?" *Well, my blood pressure is up, my intolerance for rudeness is up, and your insurance rates are now up. Oh, that's right! Much like your abuse of the English language, you don't have a grasp on the importance of insurance!"*

"Wazzup?" *Well, I was working my radar speed trap and wondered about your thoughts on the current Obama Administration."*

Wazzup?" *The front of your G-Ride (gangster looking car) will be soon up as it is briskly towed away to the impound year!*

- **What the driver said:** *"Wazzup, Big Blue?"*

- **What the officer heard:** *"What is happening officer? My, you look nice in that uniform. Have you been working out? I am up to no good and I hope to throw you off balance by pouring on some seemingly sweet courtesy.*

  *Check it out, One-Time (officer), even when I try to be nice ... it comes out like gutter gangster rap. I'm so nice ... on Mother's Day I bought my mom a Mutha-F*ing (term of endearment) Tickler Bouquet, complete with Tech-9mm Strap (a gun) and an ice cold OE 800 Malt Liquor – Vintage 2010. I'm a good homeboy, blue ... just asks my cousin (Cousin indicates anyone in the car at the time).*

- **Final Thought:** Yes, this was a white guy.

EXCUSE NUMBER 25

*When stopped for suspicion of drunk driving,
the driver stated,*

"I've been painting all day with oil-based paint and not drinking."

Risk Rating: Moderate Risk - Three Donuts

A So-So Excuse to Use on 5-0

Wow, this was a good one. Officer 5-0 mentally reviewed his law enforcement training, recent court decisions, and past experience, wondering; *"Is it possible, the smell and slur, all because of oil-based paint fumes?"* Then he looked closer. *"Hmm, Nacho cheese residue on the driver's chest, a spot of urine on his jeans, and a dozen empty beer cans on the floor – of the non oil-based variety."* Also, it's doubtful *"oil-based paint fumes"* had anything to do with recently dated divorce papers in the passenger seat, the sleeping bag in the back of the truck, and the VHS movie on the seat entitled, *"Croatian Mail Carriers Gone Wild."*

This whole picture escalated this excuse to *"No Donut - Step out of the car!"*

- **What the driver said:** *"I've been painting all day with oil-based paint and not drinking."*

- **What the officer heard:** *"I'm drunk and I just stated a truth to camouflage a lie. Yes, I've been painting all day. That means I'm a contractor or a subcontractor and statistically, we drink a lot. I then immediately tried to say I haven't been drinking – that means I have been drinking.*

  I have nothing to go home to except unpaid bills and an overused VHS player. My one-room apartment smells like bad beer and Christmas tree Air Freshener. Officer, please save me and book my ass into jail for the night."

EXCUSE NUMBER 26

After stopping a car for driving the wrong way in the Express Lanes – against the red caution arrows, the officer asked the driver, "Didn't you see the red arrows?" Driver:

"Arrows? Hell, I didn't even see the red Indians."

Risk Rating: High Risk - One Donut

Your Excuse Sucks & You're at Risk ... until:

Whoa, lone ranger! This excuse gets a "high" rating because of the extreme danger within the violation - followed by a toxic attempt at Indian humor. Poor form! Also, if the officer happens to be Native American, these words are more than simple humor! In this case, the conversation didn't get any better.

This driver laughed, chuckled, snorted and howled as the officer described the near-fatal risk of wrong-way driving. Enough is enough and off to the booking desk they went. This driver blew a .24 on the Breathalyzer (three times the level for being legally drunk).

- **What the driver said:** *Arrows? Hell, I didn't even see the red Indians."*

- **What the officer heard:** *"I'm really funny when I'm drunk. I'm so funny I have no thought process or timing associated with my wacko laugh box of a brain. I laugh at everything* *when I'm juiced; jokes, ha-ha-ha, videos of grown men being hit in the nuts with a baseball, Oh, ho-ho-hee-hee, the death of Princess Diane, HA-HA-Snort-Slobber-hee-hee, children with cancer, Oh that's a good one, HA-HA-HO-SNORT-DROOL, a head on collision with a van full of girl scouts, Oh, stop, my sides, oh my, that's a good one."*

- **Final thought:** *The judge was not laughing when the officer played the video during the trial.*

EXCUSE NUMBER 27

*When involved in a car versus pedestrian accident,
the driver stated,*

"The guy ran right out in front of me. I didn't have a chance to stop."

Risk Rating: No Donut - Step out of the car!

You Probably Blew It! Good Luck!

You are not going to believe this! The driver in this case was very convincing as he described the situation. He stated he was looking for a parking area near a sporting event and was having difficulty due to the *"fog and poor signage on the roadway."* As he navigated the foggy venue, the pedestrian ran in front of his car and was struck.

Here's the clincher: The *"pedestrian"* was actually an athlete. The *"roadway"* was actually the quarter mile running track INSIDE the stadium. Yes, this drunk had made it through the stadium gate and drove directly onto the track, running over a track star warming up for his event. The *"fog"* was a windshield sullied by cigarette smoke and compounded by a broken defroster. Thankfully, the injuries to the runner were non-life threatening.

If this driver wasn't drunk already, he should probably consider getting drunk. He really did it to himself and the poor runner.

- **What the driver said:** *"The guy ran right out in front of me. I didn't have a chance to stop."*

- **What the officer heard:** *"Officer, this stadium crowd is about to kill me and I need to be whisked away to jail for my own protection, ASAP!"*

EXCUSE NUMBER 28

When stopped after driving (and weaving) the wrong way on a one-way street, the driver stated,

"Why are you stopping me? Look at all the people driving the wrong way."

Risk Rating: No Donut - Step out of the car!

You Probably Blew It! Good Luck!

This guy is yet another example of a marginal brain under the authority of King Alcohol. It's amazing what the world looks like through the lens of toxicity. Even more amazing, these folks actually believe what they're saying. This is your brain…This is your brain speaking when you're stupid drunk. Any questions?

- **What the driver said:** *"Why are you stopping me? Look at all the people driving the wrong way."*

- **What the officer heard:** *"The world is wrong and I am right. I have a sense of entitlement - drunk and sober - and was never disciplined as a small child. Please give me the spanking I never received in my younger days." Ah, thank you!"*

EXCUSE NUMBER 29

*When stopped for a verbal warning because of a
burned-out rear light, the driver stated,*

"What the F*@# are you stopping me for?"

Risk Rating: No Donut – Step out of the car!

You Definitely Blew It! Good Luck!

It *WAS* going to be a minor traffic stop and a friendly
verbal warning. It is *NOW* a battle of right and wrong.
Why-oh-why would a person take a minor situation and
make it this major? The police often stop a driver *only*
to let him or her know something is wrong with the car.
I don't know how this driver, with his anal attitude, ever
made it this far.

- **What the driver said:** *"What the F*@# are you
  stopping me for?"*

- **What the officer heard:** *"Officer, I'm a jerk
  and I have no self control. In fact, I use my
  personality for contraception. No rubbers
  needed – just open my mouth and never have
  to worry about an unplanned pregnancy or
  STDs. I also never have to worry about getting
  gifts, Christmas cards, or phone calls.*

  *Yep! Everyone hates me because I'm an AKC
  Registered, purebred butt wipe. You, Mr.*

Officer, don't have enough tickets in that ticket book to change my venomous little tongue or attitude. You might as well get on that little police boy radio of yours and have someone bring you a fresh new ticket book."

- **Final thought:** *"Great idea! Consider it done. Another ticket book is on its way."*

EXCUSE NUMBER 30

A driver proceeded into heavy traffic from a stop sign and caused a multi-car accident. The excuse given,

"I'd waited long enough."

Risk Rating: No Donut - Step out of the car!

You Probably Blew It! Good Luck!

My, my, my, aren't you a little pocket of love and spirituality. Wow! Friends shouldn't let friends drive stressed. The news is full of reports on the U.S.'s stressed-out driving population. This driver told the truth. He was tired of waiting; he'd had enough. A lot of drivers on our streets are stressed to the max, flipped out, wigged-out, tighter than a high "C" piano wire, about to bust, or, as NASA would say, "*They lost a few thermal tiles on the re-entry.*"

According to some study (I just made up), one in five drivers are under the influence of adrenaline producing stress. Watch yourself!

- **What the driver said:** *"I'd waited long enough."*

- **What the officer heard:** *"I wonder how long you will have to wait for a bail Bondsman. Oh wait, I know ... I'll probably have to wait long enough."*

EXCUSE NUMBER 31

When stopped at 2:30 A.M., highly intoxicated, driving a RIDING LAWN MOWER, the driver stated,

"Officer, last time you threw me in jail, you said I can't drive <u>MY CAR</u> anymore."

Risk Rating: Step off the mower!

Drunks are a lot like raising a baby. They drool, mess their shorts, have trouble standing, and definitely don't always understand simple instructions. Police officers have to be sooooo careful with their words. When we way, *"You're drunk, don't drive,"* or *"You don't have a license, don't drive,"* we mean *DON'T DRIVE ANYTHING* – a lawn mower, motorcycle, golf cart, commercial airliner, passenger train, Valdez oil barge, or a Space Shuttle! No means no!

- **What the driver said:** *"Officer, last time you threw me in jail, you said I can't drive my car anymore."*

- **What the officer heard:** *"Throw away the key to the mower, my truck, my wife's truck, my girlfriend's car, and the key for my son's tricycle. Most of all throw away the key to the jail once you tuck me in for the night."*

- **Final thought:** *This was the first time in the history of this agency that they called a tow truck to impound a riding lawn mower!*

EXCUSE NUMBER 32

When stopped for speeding, the panicked driver said,

"I'm trying to get my sick parrot to the vet."

Risk Rating: Yes! Five Donuts! - Low Risk!

A Fantastic Excuse to Use on *THE MAN*

This was a *Five Donut* excuse only because the driver was telling the truth. During a closer look, the officer noticed a wrinkle newspaper on the front seat. On the paper was a pile of green and yellow feathers with what looked like two stiff birdie legs sticking up in the air. The officer decided to let the vet break the bad news of the parrot's demise to the driver. She was sent away with a warning, "*Slow down, and get that dead Polly to the vet.*"

- **What the driver said:** *"I'm trying to get my sick parrot to the veterinarian."*

- **What the officer heard:** *"I'm eccentric, unconventional, and exotic – just like my dead bird. I'm of no risk to you or the general public. I'm a little strange; however, I'm very honest."*

- **Final thought:** *Don't use regular newspaper to line the bird cage. It may be toxic. I don't know if it's the ink or something about the stories in the news, but Polly want a cracker, not a newspaper.*

EXCUSE NUMBER 33

When stopped for speeding (75 in a 55 MPH zone),
the driver stated,

"I bought my gas in Canada, so I don't have to go YOUR speed limit."

Risk Rating: Yes! Five Donuts! - Low Risk!

A Fantastic Excuse to Use on *THE MAN*

This driver *earned* a warning with this creative tour de force. Said with a smile on the driver's face, the excuse was witty and full of first-class absurdity. 5-0 gets enough downbeat compost from drivers who can't handle authority, so when we hear something as amusing as this excuse, we're appreciative and often obliged to let you go.

- **What the driver said:** *"I bought my gas in Canada, so I don't have to go YOUR speed limit."*

- **What the officer heard:** *"I am smart, sober, and want to lighten your day."*

- **Final thought:** *The officer howled about this gem for weeks!*

EXCUSE NUMBER 34

When stopped for speeding and improper lane changing, the driver stated,

"My brakes are bad. I'm just trying to get home."

Risk Rating: High Risk - One Donut

Your Excuse Sucks & You're at Risk

While the officer had to stop and think about this line, her mental process concluded with two big letters, BS! Using this excuse is like going to a benefit dinner for the NRA while wearing a tee shirt that says *I Love the ACLU*. Yes, it is your right; however, it just doesn't make sense and may be unsafe. If you use this excuse, your car will probably be towed away as hazardous. Remember, Officer Po-Po is not dumb. Don't fool yourself.

- **What the driver said:** *"My brakes are bad. I'm just trying to get home."*

- **What the officer heard:** *"My brakes are bad because I have to constantly slam them through the floorboard every time I see the police. My brakes have been bad for about four years, just like my belts, hoses, driver's license, insurance, and my tax reporting."*

EXCUSE NUMBER 35

A car manned only by a dog hit another car. The driver was found two blocks from the accident scene and explained,

"I just got this dog from the Humane Society. He went crazy and started biting me and I had to jump out of the car."

Risk Rating: Yes! Five Donuts! - Low Risk!

A Fantastic Excuse to Use on *THE MAN*

I was directly involved in this accident investigation. If I hadn't been, I would likely not believe the account. This driver left the dog pound with his cute new dog, a Rott-Satan mix, and then went to Pet's and Pals to stock up on $300 worth of leashes, collars, a doggie bed, etc. At a stop light, the excited owner decided to put the collar on his new friend. The Rott-Satan doggie went ballistic, biting, slobbering, and snarling!

Seems the collar brought back some bad memories from a meth lab or something. He bit the driver ... let's say ... in some fairly sensitive spots. The driver said, *"I'm out of here"* and bailed!

Once the dog had commandeered the car, Rott-Satan was able to pilot the rig for about 120 yards. Then it hit another car, driven by an elderly woman, head-on.

Physically, she was okay, but mentally, that's another story. Now, **every time** she sees a dog in a car, she slams on her brakes, pulls to the right shoulder, and mumbles, "*Good boy. Stay. Whoa, Good boy, Stay.*" It ain't pretty.

- **What the driver said:** *"I just got this dog from the Humane Society. He went crazy and started biting me and I had to jump out of the car."*

- **What the officer heard:** *The truth!*

- **Final thought:** *The dog's attitude did not change as he continued to cause problems for the officers and the Animal Control dude. If this ever happens to you, please aim your car for the nearest body of water or at least set the parking brake before you bail!*

- **What the Human Society said:** *"I'm sorry we have __a no return policy__ on all pets ... specifically, THAT pet!"*

EXCUSE NUMBER 36

When stopped for speeding, the middle aged woman pleaded,

"I have to go pee really bad."

Risk Rating: Moderate Risk - Three Donuts

A So-So Excuse to Use on 5-0

We have definitely heard this one a time or two. It's rated "*moderate*" because it depends on the officer's disposition at the time and how true to life the driver is. If there's a burst risk, most officers will move quickly. However, cops know you've had this bladder all your life. You knew your limits. So, excuse the pun, but if you don't schedule potty stops, this sounds like *piss poor planning* to me. That was a good one, eh? ... *Piss poor planning* ... Man, I'm funny.

Now, if you have 13 empty beer cans on the floor, you can just sit there and pee all over yourself. Remember, CONTEXT – the officer is looking at the whole picture. If you are driving home – you are likely to get a pee break from the officer. If evidence indicates you just left your house and the bathroom in your house, the tavern, or a friend's house, a pee break is not likely. It's all based on the context.

- **What the driver said:** *"I have to go pee really bad."*

- **What the officer heard:** *"I'm somewhat irresponsible and/or have a medical condition. Either way, I have to go pee really bad. I might be lying to you, but prove it. PROVE that I don't have to pee really bad. Just how long do you want to wait, Mr. 5-0? And what will we be waiting for ... to see me wet myself?*

  *How will that look in the daily news **'Officer Stands by and Waits as Mother of Three Pees Herself.'** Oh, I have another idea to prove the validity of my piss poor excuse. Follow me to a Gas Station and watch me pee. Another good headline, **'Officer Watches Mother of Three Pee.'** I didn't think so. You have a nice day too. Bye-bye."*

- **Final thought:** *This excuse pisses me off. We cannot win with this one; however, you can!*

EXCUSE NUMBER 37

After hearing the explanation of the list of traffic violations, the driver (who was the only one in the car) asked,

"Who, me?"

Risk Rating: Moderate Risk - Three Donuts

A So-So Excuse to Use on 5-0

Ah ha! Back to childhood regression at its best as we process another stressful, child-like response! This excuse is rated "*moderate*" because we've heard it many times before and can have fun with it. For instance:

Driver: "**Who me**?" Officer: "*No, not you, sir. I was talking to your invisible friend, Casper, and all the other friendly ghosts in the back seat.*" At this point a quick witted driver should say: "*You guys hold it down back there!*"

- **What the driver said:** "*Who, me?*"

- **What the officer heard:** "*I'm fairly nervous and I'm reacting normally. I'm nervous because I care; care about what you think, care about what you are about to do, and care about my insurance rates. 'Who me' was just my way of saying all of the above.*"

- **Final thought:** *Make a quick correction if you catch yourself saying something silly like, "Who Me." Amend your comment with something like, "I can't believe I just said that." The officer will chuckle and you will increase your chances of driving away ticket-free.*

EXCUSE NUMBER 38

A driver ran a red light and slammed into another car.
At the scene of the accident, the driver claimed,

"The Achilles in my right foot just snapped."

Risk Rating: Yes! Five Donuts! - Low Risk!

A Fantastic Excuse to Use on *THE MAN*

Ouch! This is an authentic, original, and a bona fide excuse (with some limitations). Yes, this Five Donut expression is the freshest in the bakery when used properly! Why? It's because this defense is possible and often too time consuming to disprove. Some States even allow these excuses as a legal defense, whereby a driver causes an accident because of unknown medical problems. The important part is it needs to be an ***unknown medical condition*** *(AKA: not known prior to the accident).*

Voluntary intoxication, the pain and itch of hemorrhoid tissue, or lead-in-the-foot are not *unknown medical conditions*. The excuse should be plausible, unlike, *"Oh my God! I rear ended the car because I was scratching mine!"* Come on! Get real! One impatient driver ran a red light after waiting fifteen seconds and claimed it was because he had Attention Deficit Disorder (ADD)! Give me a break.

- **What the driver said:** *"The Achilles in my right foot just snapped."*

- **What the officer heard:** *"I am in so much pain right now you don't want to screw with me. Let's talk more at the Emergency Room."*

- **Final thought:** *Don't lie. Danno will often follow you to the ER and will get an expert opinion from the doctor before a decision is made on the ticket.*

EXCUSE NUMBER 39

*After being stopped for spinning tires and speeding,
the driver stated,*

"Officer, I did that because I want to meet your partner."

Risk Rating: High Risk - One Donut

Your Excuse Sucks & You're at Risk

There are a couple of problems with this excuse. First of all, come to a police station, donut shop, or the annual ball if you want to meet a cop. Male and females alike use this excuse. It's akin to a driver sliding her skirt up the knee or a driver unbuttoning his shirt to expose his chest hair and spanking new medallion ... just as the officer walks up to the car. Secondly, you've created a conflict between the two officers and one is likely pissed off. You want to meet his partner? Poor form! Try some non-discriminatory sucking up by complimenting both officers.

Either way, you've given the officers something to talk about over coffee, but you haven't avoided a ticket. Keep the alluring and flirting off the streets. This is a risky excuse that may not work.

- **What the driver said:** *"Officer, I did that because I want to meet your partner."*

- **What the officer heard:** *"Officer, your partner is hot! You are a little dork and I am using you to get to your stud-of-a-cop passenger. I can see why he picked you as a patrol partner – he looks all the better when compared to your homely face. Please introduce me to your friend once you finish writing my ticket. No wait, I prefer threes. I love the number three … it has always been my lucky number. Please write me three tickets."*

EXCUSE NUMBER 40

After a car hit a tree, the driver exclaimed,

"I only had a couple of beers, but I did take five Oxys."

Risk Rating: No Donut - Step out of the car!

You Probably Blew It! Good Luck!

It's remarkable how straightforward a driver can be after a near-death experience. Also surprising are the number of people operating vehicles while under the influence of prescription (Rx) drugs and/or alcohol. Drunken driving laws also apply to being under the influence of prescriptions – your own Rx pills and those you've stolen from your grandmother. So, if you're going to take Oxycontin and have a few stiff drinks, don't drive.

Consider a designate - someone else to drive, someone who's having a drug-free time or has a more managed, responsible lifestyle. Oh, never mind ...what was I thinking; trying to find a responsible person to hang out with is always difficult when you're stealing and consuming stolen prescription drugs.

- **What the driver said:** *"I only had a couple of beers, but I did take five Oxys."*

- **What the officer heard:** *"I am chemically dependent and not likely to change myself unless I get my ass kicked - via the law. I am normally not this honest, but I'm pretty open and loving when higher than a space station. Please search my purse, my car, and my special spots. By the way, the weed under the left-rear seat is not mine and the Oxys in my purse were planted there by someone else."*

- **Final thought:** *Here's a good rule of thumb for mixing Rx drugs and booze:*

    o *1 Rx + 3 Beers + Driving = Jail*

    o *3 Rx + 2 Beers + Driving = Jail*

    o *5 Rx + 1 Cocktail + Driving = Jail*

    o *7 Rx + Um, + Uh = What is my name and how did you get into my bed?*

- **Bottom line:** *Don't do it! It's going to eventually lead to a fatality – to you, or worse, to someone else!*

EXCUSE NUMBER 41

When stopped for doing a U-turn in the middle of the street, the driver stated,

"You can't write me a ticket for that."

Risk Rating: High Risk - One Donut

Your Excuse Sucks & You're at Risk

Oh yeah. Telling a police officer what they cannot do is like boasting to the officer about your Platinum Membership with the ACLU. When you say *"you can't"* to an officer you might as well be criticizing their mothers. For the most part, officers *know* what they can or can't do on a traffic stop.

Trying to bully or intimidate an officer doesn't work. It's like telling the IRS they can't audit you. They can and work even harder when they hear the word *"can't."*

- **What the driver said:** *"You can't write me a ticket for that."*

- **What the officer heard:** *"Officer, please do a full safety and equipment inspection on my car and find all possible violations.*

- **Final thought:** *Rule of thumb: You can't say* **Never** *and never say you* **Can't** *to a police officer in his official role unless darn sure of yourself!*

EXCUSE NUMBER 42

When stopped for speeding (clocked 82 in a 55 MPH zone), the driver claimed,

"My speedometer is broken."

Risk Rating: High Risk - One Donut

Your Excuse Sucks & You're at Risk

This driver just bought another ticket — one for defective equipment. We might believe this statement if a driver deviated *slightly* from the posted speed limit. This driver, however, nearly sucked the trooper right off his radar perch on the side of the road as he went by. If your car is mistaken for a low-flying aircraft, it doesn't matter if your speedometer is broken. Get it fixed...you need it!

- **What the driver said:** *"My speedometer is broken."*

- **What the officer heard:** *"I have no idea how fast I was going and have no defense if we go to court. Write me. It is a slam dunk win in court."*

- **Final thought:** *Your defense if very weak if you had prior knowledge of broken equipment on or in your vehicle. It is better to be "surprised" by the "broken speedometer" or about whatever malfunction led to the traffic stop.*

EXCUSE NUMBER 43

When stopped for a 15 mph over in a school zone,
the driver stated,

"Sweetie, remember who butters your bread."

Risk Rating: High Risk - One Donut

Your Excuse Sucks & You're at Risk

I'm guessing this driver is saying she pays the officer's wages through taxes. If so, the most common police response is normally something like, *"Then give me a raise."* We're not concerned with a driver cutting off our take-home pay so don't even go there unless you want a souvenir in the form of a ticket. Police understand it can be ego-deflating when the men and women your tax money supports end up protecting you from yourself.

I have a suggestion that may help. Look at this occasion as you would a visit to the proctologist: It's humiliating, it hurts like hell, it's necessary, and you KNOW you're getting your money's worth. Feel better?

Another thought on this excuse … be cautious with the nicknames! Calling an officer by a pet name is hazardous to your pocketbook. *"Sweetie, honey, love button, golden cheeks, child, boy, and baby"* move you into hazardous LOW DONUT territory. Common courtesy is always safe.

- **What the driver said:** *"Sweetie, remember who butters your bread."*

- **What the officer heard:** *"You're dead wrong officer and you're messing with the wrong person. Because I pay taxes I have the right to blast through a school zone at any speed I see fit. I really want and need a ticket."*

EXCUSE NUMBER 44

Following a high-speed pursuit involving five police cars and the driver was suspected of being drunk, the driver explained,

"I thought you were my wife."

Risk Rating: No Donut - Step out of the car!

You Probably Blew It! Good Luck!

I know what you're thinking … why would his wife be chasing him? Does his wife have a siren and red and blue lights on her minivan? Does his wife have four friends with additional police cars that also chase him? Hard to believe someone actually said this, but it's true. This driver repeated the same statement over and over all the way to jail. By morning, however, when he'd sobered up, the excuse changed dramatically: *"I did what? No way!"*

Police run into the worst of society and we run into the *best* of society at their temporary worst. Add alcohol and drugs to either and you have a volatile mix of trouble. A better excuse for this driver would have been, *"Who me?"*

- **What the driver said:** *"I thought you were my wife."*

- **What the officer heard:** *"I'm drunk. In addition to my wife, I'm also in trouble in a number of different areas of my life. My wife is simply symbolic of how screwed up my life has become. Officer, I need your help and protection. Can I have a room for the night?"*

EXCUSE NUMBER 45

When stopped for going double the posted speed limit in a construction zone, the driver asked,

"What's the matter, don't you have your quota?"

Risk Rating: Higher than High Risk – One Donut

Your Excuse Sucks & You're at Risk

This guy failed in originality and attitude. Feel free to slam the police with comments like this, but come up with some new material. This is right up there with, *"Sweetie, remember who butters your bread."* The quota-quip was popular in the 70's and has slowly lost steam since. This driver has earned a ticket before the officer said a word. He's probably earned more than one ticket.

Here are some of our favorite responses to a moronic statement like this:

Officer: "Nope, no quota, but I do get a feeling of superiority in doing this."

Officer: "Actually, I already have my quota, but for you I'll write extras."

Officer: "I have no quota. I'm going to write you as many tickets as I want."

Officer: "This will make my quota, thanks for screwing up."

Officer: "Yes, in fact, if I give you three tickets, I get a free IPod."

Most police agencies *do not* have quotas. But if you happen to be in a district that does and you say this, chances are the officer will meet his or her quota by writing you tickets. So why say it?

- **What the driver said:** *"What's the matter? Don't you have your quota?"*

- **What the officer heard:** *"I'm a smart ass and I'm trying to immediately transfer blame to you, Mister Officer. Hey, police-boy, there's only one way to balance the scales of power and check my ego – write me a few tickets. Because I'm such an ass, I will likely not sign the tickets. This will give you the pleasure of saying No Donut – Step out of the car."*

EXCUSE NUMBER 46

When stopped in the inner city for running stop lights, the driver claimed,

"I'm lost. I gotta get out of this place."

Risk Rating: Yes! Five Donuts! - Low Risk!

A Fantastic Excuse to Use on *THE MAN*

If the context matches the words, this is a great excuse. This actually happens quite often in LA, Detroit, Houston, and the White House. A lot of good people from the suburbs get lost in a crime riddled inner city. Hopefully, if you use this excuse, the cop will be understanding and help you along the way. *But,* if the officer recognizes you from the 'hood (as one she sees over and over again), and you're lying - you're in deep ... well, I'll put it this way. The jail now takes Visa, Master Card and American Express. Make sure you have your cards with you and ensure your name is on the credit card.

- **What the driver said:** *"I'm lost. I gotta get out of this place."*

- **What the officer heard:** *"I'm honest and I gotta get out of this place."*

EXCUSE NUMBER 47

When stopped for improper lane travel and for running a stop sign, the driver stated,

"Me speeka noooo inglish."

Risk Rating: Moderate Risk - Three Donuts

A So-So Excuse to Use on 5-0

If you really have a license and really are challenged by the English language, this is a safe excuse. Typically, an officer's first thought upon hearing this excuse is, *"then howa deed ya geet a licenseeo?"* (The Department of Licensing seems to hand them out like baseball cards.) Sure, an officer will consider this possibility when he or she hears this statement. The person really might not understand English.

An officer usually translates this excuse into *"Please searcha mee car."* And, depending upon what border we're nearest, he will search very carefully. Everyone's welcome to Mother America, but if they have three pounds of cocaine in the trunk, some high explosives, or if they are faking their knowledge of the English language, then improper lane travel becomes painfully serious.

- **What the driver said:** *"Me speeka noooo inglish."*

- **What the officer heard:** *"Me need a lot more attention before you let me go. Me need a full records check. Me need a Homeland Security check. Me need an Interpol Persons Search. Me have nothing to do for the next 45 minutes. What a Contree."*

EXCUSE NUMBER 48

When stopped for a series of traffic violations,
the driver asked,

"Do you know Officer Stevens and Captain Minks?"

Risk Rating: High Risk - One Donut

Your Excuse Sucks & You're at Risk

While this may seem natural, it is nothing more than name droppings. Please be careful when you try this. Yes, I said name ***droppings*** for a reason – as in poop. This is the big one for a traffic cop and happens nearly every day.

No one likes someone who drops a name in the climax of trouble. What in the heck has Officer Stevens got to do with this driver's sloppy driving? It really gets tense when the driver claims to know an officer and the officer is the one who made the stop. You messed up; accept what's coming.

- **What the driver said:** *"Do you know Officer Stevens and Captain Minks?"*

- **What the officer heard:** *"Did you know I lack accountability for my actions? I pray that you know Officer Stevens or Captain Minks. Oh, goodness gracious! You ARE Officer Stevens, how long has it been? Oh, golly, we've never* met? Really? No wait, didn't we meet at the ACLU luncheon last month? What's that? Step out of the car?"

- **Final thought:** *Name droppings belong in a litter box. Don't do it!*

EXCUSE NUMBER 49

When stopped for improper lane travel and speeding, the driver claimed,

"My Menstrual Cycle just started and I'm not prepared."

Risk Rating: Yes! Five Donuts! - Low Risk!

A Fantastic Excuse to Use on *THE MAN*

Oh boy, this one's a keeper! It's a beautiful thing any time a driver can effectively use a taboo topic on one of us. This excuse makes everyone uncomfortable and it's difficult to disprove. Ever since childhood this subject has been taboo, especially for men. So, most cops won't want to launch into a long dissertation. Besides, what are we going to say anyway? *"Yeah, right lady, I really don't think you're starting to menstruate."*

- **What the driver said:** *"My Menstrual Cycle just started and I'm not prepared."*

- **What the officer heard:** *"Officer, you are in delicate territory. You're at risk in a number of areas. The best thing to do is keep your ink pen in its holster, explain that you stopped the wrong car, and quietly drive away. Don't worry, I won't tell anyone and I know you won't bring it up in the police locker room."*

- **Final thought:** *This is an awesome excuse; however, be cautious not to use it more than once a month.*

EXCUSE NUMBER 50

*When stopped for speeding and a stop sign violation,
the young driver stated,*

"I'm sorry, but I've got pizzas to deliver."

Risk Rating: Moderate Risk - Three Donuts

A So-So Excuse to Use on 5-0

Again, this is a fairly good excuse considering the context. This kid is being honest and we understand the pressure these young kids work under. For minimum wage, they're required to deliver these pizzas within a short time frame.

A recent court decision held a large pizza company responsible for encouraging young drivers to speed to keep their advertised *"Fast Delivery"* promise. Several accidents resulted and the company was held liable for Gazillion dollars (that's a lot of pizza, but I prefer donuts).

Often, the driver will get a pass and the officer will look for any future speeding patterns of this particular pizza delivery company.

- **What the driver said:** *"I'm sorry, but I've got pizzas to deliver."*

- **What the officer heard:** *"I'm honest, I'm underpaid, and I'm over-stressed."*

- **Final thought:** *Officers love kids and others who are trying to make a living.*

EXCUSE NUMBER 51

*When stopped for suspicion of drunk driving,
the driver stated,*

**"I'm really F*@#d up. I deserve to
be arrested."**

Risk Rating: No Donut - Step out of the car!

You Probably Blew It! Good Luck!

Thank you for the honesty, pickle head. Too little – too late! Throwing one's self on the mercy of the cop doesn't work the way it does for the court. This driver might have done better to throw himself on the mercy of someone to drive him home. Admissions are empty, once your head is marinated and you're behind the wheel.

The officer can usually tell how messed up a person is without help from the driver. Typically, we've been observing the frolics of a car driven by someone with a contaminated brain for quite awhile. We have a clue how messed up that person is before we pull him or her over.

Thanks for the truth, but there's no need to tell us; breathing anywhere near us does the job.

- **What the driver said:** *"I'm really F*@#d up. I deserve to be arrested."*

- **What the officer heard:** *"I'm pitifully drunk and I will always confess once all the evidence has been presented. Yes, I'm the type of guy who waits until his wife catches him in bed with the neighbor to say, 'Oh honey, I'm sorry, but I've been telling you all along that I'm not happy with our marriage.'*

  Honey, since I'm confessing, do you remember that time I said 'I'm just helping the sheep over the fence?' Well, actually ..."

EXCUSE NUMBER 52

*When stopped for speeding on a beautiful Tuesday
afternoon, the driver stated,*

"I'm not signing any tickets!"

Risk Rating: High Risk - One Donut

Your Excuse Sucks & You're at Risk

Good answer, Ace. Traffic officers get this everyday all
over the country – in large and small communities
alike. It's a great thing to say if you don't have
anything to do for the next twenty-four hours.

Now, at this point, she will present a driver with the
ticket anyway and give him or her ample time to sign it.
If the driver still refuses to sign, the risk jumps to *"No
donut, step out of the car."* The driver has now earned
a guaranteed trip to jail. Remember, you do have
rights; however, not signing the ticket will get you
booked.

- **What the driver said:** *"I'm not signing any
  tickets!"*

- **What the officer heard:** *"I have rights! I'm not
  signing squat and I will roll up my window and
  hold my breath. One of my rights is to have you
  drag me out of my car and book my ass into jail.
  That's right police-girl, I dare you! Go ahead,
  take your best shot. Ouch! Owee! Okay, now
  I'll sign the ticket. What? Too late?"*

- **Final thought:** *Sign the ticket. It is a promise to respond and an agreement that you will not ignore the situation - not an admission of guilt.*

EXCUSE NUMBER 53

When stopped for improper lane travel and suspicion of drunk driving, the driver stated,

"Believe me, Baby ... I drive better when I'm a bit tipsy!"

Risk Rating: No Donut - Step out of the car!

You Probably Blew It! Good Luck!

What the blanket-blank-blank? The driver tried this excuse hoping to catch the officer off guard. It worked…for a second. Then the officer asked the driver, *"Let's see what else you're better at drunk."* Guess what? The driver wasn't any better at walking on a white line, touching the tip of his nose, reciting the ABC's, or holding one foot off the ground.

There is a myth that our golf game, softball, pool, darts, or other sports might be enhanced with alcohol, but the truth remains, driving *is not*! The other problem with this excuse is that it gives a person a rationale to drive drunk. Not a good thing to tell a cop.

- **What the driver said:** *"Believe me, Baby ... I drive better when I'm a bit tipsy!"*

- **What the officer heard:** *"I'm delusional and called you 'Baby.' Book me!"*

- **Final thought:** *The belief "I'm better after a few drinks" is still quite common.*

EXCUSE NUMBER 54

A driver living in Washington State was stopped with no valid Washington State driver's license. A computer check showed the person to have a suspended driver's license in Oregon. When asked about this predicament, the driver explained,

"Officer, why in the hell would I get a license in Washington after the State of Oregon took mine away?"

Risk Rating: Moderate Risk - Three Donuts

A So-So Excuse to Use on 5-0

Even though I might not agree with this driver's rationale, I had to give him a *"moderate"* rating for effort. A statement made with this much commitment (from the heart) compels an officer to act out of compassion for the driver's ignorance. The driver obviously mistook the purpose of a driver's license suspension. What's there to learn from this, fella? Wonder if he also thinks the purpose of family reunions is to pick up on girls?

- **What the driver said:** *"Officer, why in the hell would I get a license in Washington after the State of Oregon took mine away?"*

- **What the officer heard:** *"I'm honest and a little ignorant."*

EXCUSE NUMBER 55

When stopped for running a red light, the driver stated,

"Officer, the light was really orange."

Risk Rating: High Risk - One Donut

Your Excuse Sucks & You're at Risk

I guess this is mind over matter. You pull up to a light – cycling from yellow to red - and begin to visualize it as orange. Focus now. Focus. You can see an orange traffic light instead of a red one. *Orange, orange.* No, *Red.* No, *Orange!* Whoa, denial is at work in your life and behind the wheel!

When you've cut off your arm and it's spewing arterial blood all over the kitchen or the shop – do you say *"No big deal, it's orange blood, not red. Don't put any pressure on the wound, it's just orange. Wait until it turns red, and then we'll talk about stopping it. No worries … just orange."* Now, please explain this to the rest of the world. What difference does it make whether the light was red or a beautiful orange pumpkin color? *Stop* at the stinking light. And have your eyes checked.

- **What the driver said:** *"Honest, Officer, the light was really orange."*

- **What the officer heard:** *"I'm full of sh*!, um, I mean denial, I'm dangerous and I fudge on everything … just a tad."*

EXCUSE NUMBER 56

*When stopped and told of a series of traffic violations
he'd committed, the driver responded,*

"You don't know what you're talking about."

Risk Rating: High Risk - One Donut

Your Excuse Sucks & You're at Risk

Remember when you took the trip into the human body
during health and science class in 10th grade? Yes?
Okay, let's go into the body of the traffic cop who just
heard this justification. The pulse quickens, raising the
blood pressure twenty-five marks. A squirt of
adrenaline releases into the bloodstream, enhancing
vision and mental powers. Muscles tense, preparing
the body for combat. The mind flashes back to long
hours in college and the police academy. From the
deepest depths of the officer's soul comes the internal
voice with one simple instruction: Show this S.O.B.
exactly how much you *do* know by writing him for
everything possible.

Be careful. We have lots of time, ticket books, a Load-
'O-Pens, and buckets of ink.

- **What the driver said:** *"You don't know what
  you're talking about."*

- **What the officer heard:** *"I'm a defense lawyer
  and I love to be right. Wait, strike that, I AM
  ALWAYS right! Just ask my mail ordered wife*

who is completely submissive and only speaks enough English to say, 'Yes honey' and 'Please no hit me again.'

Yes, I'm a bully behind the wheel and cannot stand the smell of authority in any form. I represent the dark side of the world and this is the only chance you will have to slay the dragon. Write me!"

- **Final thought:** *Remember to avoid these words with the officer: Can't, never, always, and you don't know what you're talking about.*

EXCUSE NUMBER 57

When stopped for speeding, the driver claimed,

"I'm a doctor. I have to get to the hospital now."

Risk Rating: Yes! Five Donuts! - Low Risk!

A Fantastic Excuse to Use on *THE MAN* ...unless

"Right away, sir!" And off we go, jumping over curbs, down hills, and screeching around corners to ensure the doctor arrives safely and quickly. While being a doctor does not give one license to break the law; most police and sheriff officials do believe in *"professional courtesy"* for these situations. We don't want to hold up a medical professional on his way to saving a life or bringing a new baby into the world. Whew, we made it to the hospital! *"There you go, sir. Good luck."*

As Paul Harvey says, "here's the rest of the story." If you use this excuse, be sure you're a doctor and be sure you have a bona-fide emergency. The officer will be checking your story. In this case, we were not dealing with a doctor. We were dealing with an X-ray Technician who was running late.

Other fictitious *"Doctor Emergencies"* have produced the following results:

- Doctors who were really *not* doctors, but played one on TV

- Doctors who had no emergencies

- A doctor who was a plastic surgeon rushing to do a routine procedure (one of my favorites). The officer told this doctor, "*Sir, I know breast implants are crucial to some people, but they don't constitute an emergency. Sign here, please.*"

- **What the driver said:** "*I'm a doctor. I have to get to the hospital now.*"

- **After getting the truth, this is what the officer heard:** "*I am irresponsible, have a time management problem, and I'm willing to lie to avoid responsibility. Officer, please let my employer know that I was escorted to my job by the police without the presence of an emergency and after lying.*"

EXCUSE NUMBER 58

*After being stopped for throwing a lit cigarette from a
new sports car, the driver stated,*

"I didn't want to get my car dirty."

Risk Rating: High Risk - One Donut

Your Excuse Sucks & You're at Risk

This makes perfectly good sense to me. We can keep
the ashtray clean by throwing our burning cigarettes
into the kiln-dry forested land. What a dork! In most
states this is a very costly traffic ticket. Some officers
will make the driver walk back and pick up the stinking,
smoldering butt rather than give him or her a ticket.

In this case, the driver was a firefighter (go figure) who
refused to pick it up. He was given the appropriate
$900 plus ticket.

The officer knew this person was a butt flicker and
believed he habitually threw lit cigarettes out the
window of his car. Why did he know? Well, anyone
with skin like the Marlboro Man and a sparkling clean
ashtray is a habitual butt thrower. The firefighter said
he *"thought"* it was legal to do so. Was it job security
or just stupidity? I don't know. As Smokey the Bear
would put it, *"Keep your butts in the car!"*

- **What the driver said:** *"I didn't want to get my car dirty."*

- **What the officer heard:** *"I'm dying from cigarette smoking and have a burning desire to take some people with me. I want to start a series of brush and forest fires in an attempt to kill as many people as possible before I go. An expensive ticket will go far in stopping me from my homicidal run."*

EXCUSE NUMBER 59

*A drunk driver, after unsuccessfully singing his
ABC's several times, he stated,*

**"Officer, this is B.S. I never learned how
to sing alphabets. You try it."**

Risk Rating: No Donut - Step out of the car!

You Probably Blew It! Good Luck!

Come on! Officers never asked anyone to sing the
ABC's. Besides, most junior colleges no longer require
knowledge of the alphabet. This excuse is incredible
and the driver won the E-ticket to the booking desk.
He's earned a trip to the slammer for sure. P.S., If
you're ever in this situation, singing the ABC's is okay.
We like it. Typically, once the officer knows you're
drunk, she will go ahead and ask you to sing it over
again. Also, a little known fact … embarrassing for
police officers … we usually hum along.

- **What the driver said:** *"Officer, this is B.S. I
  never learned how to sing alphabets. You try
  it."*

- **What the officer heard:** *"I'm drunk and a little
  pissed. I need to be booked."*

EXCUSE NUMBER 60

When stopped for running a red light,
the driver admitted,

"I don't get paid until Friday. I'm really
stupid. I can't believe I did it.
God knows, I'll pay for it."

Risk Rating: Who knows at this point

This caught the officer by surprise. What is this woman talking about? What has this got to do with running a red light? Nothing, but it gets interesting.

Fifteen minutes earlier, this driver filled her car with $21 worth of gas and drove away without paying. The gas station didn't know. No police report was filed. But, when the cop presented her with a ticket for running a red light, she confessed.

Epilogue: She still got a ticket for running a red light. Once she signed, she heard *"No Donut - Step out of the car!"* Bummer, plenty of gas and nowhere to go.

- **What the driver said:** *"I don't get paid until Friday. I'm really stupid. I can't believe I did it. God knows, I'll pay for it."*

- **What the officer heard:** *"Every time I do something wrong, I get caught. This is just another example of not being able to do* *anything crooked or criminal. God's really talking to me. In fact, God's voice will be much clearer in the quiet of my own jail cell."*

- **Final thought:** *Make sure you know what you are being stopped for before you fall on your sword.*

EXCUSE NUMBER 61

A car pulled out from a stop sign into heavy traffic and caused a multi-car accident. The driver explained,

"I made eye contact with the other driver and thought I was good to go."

Risk Rating: High Risk - One Donut

Your Excuse Sucks & You're at Risk

This stated cause of the accident was our violator's belief that he could read the eyes of another driver whom he does not know. It's tempting to ask the at-fault driver a few simple questions:

So, what was it about the other driver's eyes that made it okay to pull into the traffic moving at 45 MPH? Was it a wink? Did both of his eyes dart quickly and repeatedly to the right – saying "hey, pull out … now." Or was it one of those downward nods, with a two-eye blink-blink – like the girl on the show *I Dream of Genie.* Was it the eyes of the driver in the car closest to you? Or was it the third driver back, the fourth, or fifth car back that gave you the *"good to go"* signal?

- **What the driver said:** *"I made eye contact with the other driver and thought I was good to go."*

- **What the officer heard:** *"Officer, I was playing with my IPod, texting my wife, and trying to type my girlfriends address into my on-board navigation system. I'm too proud to tell you that*

I made a mistake. This excuse was the only thing I could pull out of my butt after the shock of the collision - besides my IPod, which I had to do some digging for."

- **Final thought:** *Honest is great; this is not the type of honesty I'm referring to.*

EXCUSE NUMBER 62

At 2:30 A.M. one-half block from a fully marked patrol car, a car rear-ended a motorist stopped at a red light. The driver of the car was suspected of being drunk, and responded,

"Of course I rear-ended the guy. I couldn't see a damned thing... I turned my lights off when I saw your patrol car."

Risk Rating: No Donut - Step out of the car,

NOW!

You Probably Blew It! Good Luck!

For us, this is sometimes quite entertaining. We watch the show – other cars flashing their brights and honking their horns at the drunk with the headlights off. And the drunk is just buzzing along, *"Doe-dee-doe-dee-dee... no one can see me. Doe-dee-doe ... I turned my lights off so the stupid little piggy can go to market instead of come to me... Doe-dee-dah."* Talk about a way to attract attention ... screaming for attention!

This isn't as weird or as unusual as it may sound. I hear of cases throughout the United States where drunk drivers turn off their headlights when they see a patrol car, even in the middle of well-lit cities. It must be some sort of bizarre alcohol-related delusion: *I can't be seen when drunk if I turn off my headlights...Doe-dee-doe!*

- **What the driver said:** *"Of course I rear-ended the guy. I couldn't see a damned thing ... I turned my lights off when I saw your patrol car."*

- **What the officer heard:** *"I'm drunk and stupid. In fact, my mother drank a lot when she was pregnant with me and my older twin brother. Doe-dee-doe."*

- **Final thought:** *If you have a relative that drinks and then sings Doe-dee-doe – grab the keys. Hell, knock him out if you need to, but don't let him drive.*

EXCUSE NUMBER 63

When stopped for rolling through a four-way stop intersection, the driver exclaimed,

"My lawyer said you can't stop me for that!"

Risk Rating: High Risk - One Donut

Your Excuse Sucks & You're at Risk

How should an officer respond to this: *"Oh, you're right, Mr. Driver, you've caught me in a ring of dark vice and sordid places. Since attending the academy, I've been sneaking around stopping cars for running stop signs. I'd hoped I'd never be caught, but you know better and it's all over for me. I may as well turn in my badge. The world's wrong and you're right!"*

Nope, the officer simply stated, *"Hey, how many tickets has your lawyer written this year?"*

Excuse my sarcasm, but what a *foolhardy thing to say to 5-0!* I don't know if the officer in this case should write the driver or slap the lawyer. Maybe she should slap both of them and write the driver. Of course, we can stop someone for this....and a bunch of other stuff too. The average driver makes a butt load of mistakes during each mile of city driving. The rolling stop is one of the many infractions. Do you want to be right or broke?

- **What the driver said:** *"My lawyer said you can't stop me for that!"*

- **What the officer heard:** *"My lawyer will also encourage me to go to court to fight this ticket. Officer, that means you will get four hours of overtime pay for a court appearance and not even need to testify. If you want to pay off that Visa Card, write me a ticket. You can also learn who my lawyer is and what type of car he drives. It's all around a good idea to write me a ticket."*

- **Final thought:** *"Lawyer" is a bad word. Just avoid using the word in the presence of the traffic cop. Exorcise it from your list of excuses. Come on, let's practice: "My Lawyer", I mean, "Oh, I didn't know that officer." Good job!*

EXCUSE NUMBER 64

When an elderly drunk driver rear-ended a car stopped
for a passing train, he claimed,

"I'm trying to find clothes. I demand
my clothing!"

Risk Rating: No Donut – Here's a blanket.

Now, step out of the car!

You Probably Blew It! Good Luck!

Initially, it was difficult to tell if this was a victim of oldness or something more serious, like a medical problem or an alcoholic blackout. Most officers have a soft spot in the heart for children and the elderly. Even after an accident, officers are known to give a break to a cute old lady or man, if and when possible.

In this case, it was not a matter of a sweet old one suffering from aging. This sixty-nine-year-old man had been driving highly intoxicated for over eighty-five miles – naked – wearing only a pair of brown dress socks and worn black leather wingtip shoes. He looked a little like my dad when he mows the lawn on Saturday mornings. But this guy's socks matched.

The arresting officer never found out what happened to the rest of his clothing, but obliged the gentleman by giving him a clean set of orange jail coveralls for the night. He looked hot in his new outfit and those black wingtips. Yow, he was quite a sight.

- **What the driver said:** *"I'm trying to find clothes. I demand my clothing!"*

- **What the officer heard:** *"I'm in trouble and if the car was not in my way I would be dead — stuck underneath the train."*

- **Final thought:** *We feel sorry for the less fortunate and the elderly … until they are drunk and dangerous!*

EXCUSE NUMBER 65

Continuing the theme of partially dressed: When stopped for speeding (51 in a 30 MPH zone) and for improper lane travel, the officer found the driver was half dressed. The driver explained,

"I'm going to dinner and I was changing my clothes."

Risk Rating: Moderate Risk - Three Donuts

A So-So Excuse to Use on 5-0

This driver was in the process of changing from her work clothes into a cocktail dress when the officer pulled her over. What's worse, she claimed she did this all the time. The officer was quite lenient, giving her a minor ticket rather than charging her with a criminal offense. But later that night he pulled over the same car and found her changing from her cocktail dress into her pajamas.

Not! I added the pajama touch for a nice ending to this true story. Sorry...I couldn't resist.

- **What the driver said:** *"I'm going to dinner and I was changing my clothes."*

- **What the officer heard:** *"While honest, I'm a very scary driver. I need a ticket because of the apparent comfort I find in my wardrobe dysfunction. Yes, I also put on eye liner while* *driving, work some pit stick deodorant into my warm spots, and I sometimes wax my legs while driving. Write me, big boy."*

- **Final thought:** *We are creatures of habit and once an officer notices a driver with a dangerous habit, action is needed and taken. Putting on makeup, shaving, and even brushing the teeth while driving is too common. Too much activity in the driver's seat will eventually lead to an accident. Stop!*

EXCUSE NUMBER 66

A truck was stopped for atrocious driving: Wrong way on a one-way street, cutting through parking lots to avoid traffic lights, and running stop signs. The officer asked the driver about the ghastly driving and the driver replied,

"I have no F*!*ing idea. Why don't YOU tell ME?"

Risk Rating: High Risk - One Donut

Your Excuse Sucks & You're at Risk

Oh boy! This sounds like the comment a 15 year old makes when caught in the act. Doesn't it? Remember getting caught as a kid and then answering to an angry adult, "*I don't know? I hate you. Leave me alone. I hate the world and you.*" It never worked for me and I doubt it will work for any of you either.

It's the same with a police officer. "*I don't know or I have no F-ng idea.*" spurns the police officer to pass out some educational motivation to the offending driver; learning through the price tag or court appearance attached. Use this excuse and you're bound to get a ticket. I also don't recommend using this excuse in a court of law. The judge will come up with an even stronger lesson. I suggest telling the truth to the police officer and the judge. The truth is rare and that means it works ... and you feel a lot better afterward.

- **What the driver said:** *"I have no F*!*ing idea. Why don't YOU tell ME.?"*

- **What the officer heard:** *"I have a chemical imbalance and need to get out of the driver's seat and into counseling. Officer, since you're not a counselor would you be kind enough to give me a front row ticket to court?*

- **Final thought:** *Be smart, be kind, and be honest. If you ask an officer to "guess" what you did — he will - and you will not be happy. Tell him what you did and you have a better chance of a warning. The truth is rare and it works because it is uncommon!*

EXCUSE NUMBER 67

*When stopped for speeding (49 in a 35 MPH zone),
the driver stated,*

"I just drove through the carwash and I'm trying to dry my car."

Risk Rating: High Risk - One Donut

Your Excuse Sucks & You're at Risk

This excuse is common during the car washing season. And it makes sense: Avoid those irritating water stains after washing your car by speed drying. No need to buy the $12 Chamois or the $8 baby diaper from the carwash vending machine. While this is understandable and blow-drying a car seems natural, it remains very dangerous. It's risky because the driver is distracted and attempting to accelerate faster and hotter than usual. During the high speed spin cycle, we are looking at the droplets on the windows and glancing at the trunk lid to check out the dehydrating progress. We are not paying attention to what's in front of us.

With that said, I do this every time I wash my car. Yes, I take part in high-risk drying habits. I'm also right next to an interstate highway and do not need to speed – too much.

P.S. Unless you're lucky enough to be pulled over by me, (not likely these days) you'll probably get a ticket for trying this stunt.

- **What the driver said:** *"I just drove through the carwash and I'm trying to dry my car."*

- **What the officer heard:** *"I'm speeding around in my wet car looking for a group of people in cotton clothing. Once I find them, I plan to mow through the crowd and complete the drying process. I've looked around in the past for some people wearing Chamois jumpsuits, but I couldn't locate anyone. I need to settle for a cotton wipe down."*

- **Final thought:** *I'm guilty and not qualified to provide a final thought on this one!*

EXCUSE NUMBER 68

A car with camping gear strapped to the top, was stopped for suspicion of drunk driving and poor lane travel in the city, the driver stated,

"Geez Officer, I'm only two blocks from home."

Risk Rating: No Donut - Step out of the car!

You Probably Blew It! Good Luck!

First of all, please stop saying this when we pull you over. It's obvious you're trying to get home because it's most likely 2:00 A.M. and you're so far gone even *Jackson L. Daniels* wouldn't serve you booze. Secondly, <u>two more blocks to go</u> doesn't mean squat to us. We're concerned with the people you've run off the road so far. In this case, camping gear indicates you've made a fairly long drive while poop-faced.

Finally, we love to make an arrest of a drunk in his or her own neighborhood.   The neighbors are usually euphoric as someone finally caught the dork that's been driving over their lawns, urinating in their driveways, and crashing into their garbage cans.

For every one arrest for driving while intoxicated, the driver has taken part in 2000 acts of actual behind-the-wheel drunk driving - undetected. So save the B.S. for your family and friends; they're probably used to it. We want you off the streets!

- **What the driver said:** *"Geez Officer, I'm only two blocks from home."*

- **What the officer heard:** *"Officer, I'm two blocks from home – now. A little while ago I was 30 miles from home and really drunk. An hour ago I was 60 miles from home and pretty damn tipsy. Two hours ago I left the campsite half in the bag and already had a pee spot on my jeans.*

  Officer, I drive drunk for a living. Yep, I'm a career drunk – diploma and everything. I brew beer, have beer on my corn flakes, and even make my hot chocolate with beer. With that said, I'm only two blocks from home."

EXCUSE NUMBER 69

Location: *Military base in a heavily forested area (broad daylight).*

Incident: *An honor student, 17, hit an armored personal carrier.*

Vehicle color: *Army Green – traditional army camouflage.*

The driver of the vehicle causing the accident claimed,

"Officer, I honestly didn't see it."

Risk Rating: Yes! Five Donuts! - Low Risk!

A Fantastic Excuse to Use on *THE MAN*

Helloooooo! Hello Uncle Sam! Does this make sense, Sammy? While hard to believe the driver never saw a five-ton greenish-colored truck, he definitely used a safe excuse! What's the purpose, painting an Army truck camouflaged green? It is painted that way to AVOID BEING SEEN!

That's right! The entire purpose of camouflaging a truck is to allow the monster to move from point A to point B without being detected. We shouldn't be surprised when our new driver slams into the rig. What are we going to say, *"Hey punk, you ran into a truck you should have seen. I know, we designed and painted it so it won't be noticed. That's irrelevant! We're the government for Pete's sake!"*

Another angle: It could get very ugly if the officer ticketed the driver for impact with the camouflaged vehicle that's painted to be undetectable. Yes, a nasty courtroom fight would probably ensue. The battle would bring back the Cold War debate, military downsizing, Iraq, and possibly more.

A $124 dollar ticket (or thereabouts) could lead to a messy multimillion dollar court battle? That camo-thingy is a trade secret. It's like Col. Sander's Secret Recipe! Let's just make this go away! Never mind!

- **What the driver said:** *"Officer, I honestly didn't see it."*

- **What the officer heard:** *"I didn't see what? Was there anything to be seen? Let's just move along, officer. Let's take this to our grave. We didn't see anything … if anything was even there."*

EXCUSE NUMBER 70

When stopped for speeding 15 over, the driver
sarcastically stated,

"Oh, I thought you just stopped me to hand out
tickets to the Policeman's Ball."

Risk Rating: High Risk - One Donut

Your Excuse Sucks & You're at Risk

Unpleasant, surly, mocking, dim-witted, and very expensive! *"Please, you're killing me. Oh, my sides, you're so funny – a famous comedian perhaps. Can I have your autograph…right here next to the line stating "Court Date?"*

Most police and sheriff's departments don't sponsor a Policeman's Ball these days. *"Uh oh, there you go again. What was that? 'Well then, Officer, is it fair to say that policemen no longer have balls?' Geez you're good. Let me get another autograph."*

- **What the driver said:** *"Oh, I thought you just stopped me to hand out tickets to the Policeman's Ball."*

- **What the officer heard:** *"If you don't have tickets to the ball, can you give me a stack of traffic tickets? Thank you, I feel better already. See you in court."*

- **Final thought:** *Remember: we love humor – watch the timing.*

EXCUSE NUMBER 71

A seventeen-year-old male was stopped for speeding and he stated,

"Officer, my girlfriend said she's ready and I'm not ... I need to buy some protection."

Risk Rating: Yes! Five Donuts! - Low Risk!

A Fantastic Excuse to Use on *THE MAN*

Officers all over the country would love to hear this excuse. Most of us classify this as "Low Risk!" because it's sincere, made in haste, and takes us back to our younger days – ah, the nostalgia of unprepared romance. Oh, those were the rebellious, wonderful days. Times have changed and we need to tolerate some unsafe driving in order to ensure safe sex.

This excuse works because it's entertaining and lighthearted, and something officers can appreciate. We get enough of the deep, profound, and uneasy waste. If you can lighten it up in good taste with an officer, you slide safely into Five Donut territory!

- **What the driver said:** *"Officer, my girlfriend said she's ready and I'm not ... I need to buy some protection."*

- **What the officer heard:** *"Officer, I'm driving like crap for a darn good reason ... safe sex! When all the blood is circulating properly to my* brain, I'm a very responsible driver. It's just that my brain is getting no blood right now and it's getting a load of new chemicals. Please give me some grace."

- **Final thought:** *I really hope he was able to complete the journey safely … heh-heh!*

Cute kid!

EXCUSE NUMBER 72

When stopped for several traffic violations, the
pregnant driver stated,

"Well, Hi There! Do you remember me?"

Risk Rating: No Rating
(and no need for a rating!)

Gulp! The officer looked at the driver, said "*Oh no,*" then walked back to his patrol car and drove away without saying another word. It seems he'd stopped the girl by accident, not knowing she was the one he had dated for a very short period of time. Um, let's just say they dated within the past nine months. Accidents do happen!

- **What the driver said:** *"Well, Hi There! Do you remember me?"*

- **What the officer heard:** *"Well, Hi There! What were you planning to do with your income for the next 18 years? Please put a little aside for OUR insignificant investment – say about one-half your annual salary. Don't worry about a name for the little blessing. The name has been selected and will be on the paternity suit that should be served soon. Bye-bye now!"*

- **Final thought:** *Officers are human and subjected to the many stressors experienced by the rest of our wonderful country. This was a significant and life altering event!*

EXCUSE NUMBER 73

An intoxicated driver was in a one-car rollover. He <u>was</u> a candidate for hire to the same law enforcement agency the traffic cop worked for. The driver asked,

"This won't hurt my chances, will it?"

Risk Rating: No Donut - Step out of the car!

You Probably Blew It! Good Luck!

Answer: *Yes, this changes things just a tad. But, thank you for your interest and good luck with your prosecution and treatment program.* The traffic cop on the scene was uncomfortable but convinced this person may want to hold off on the police career. We like to weed them out when we find them. Drunk driving is one way to lose a chance at being hired by a police agency. Other include:

- o Bringing a therapist to a police job interview.

- o Bringing your mom and dad with you - the first day on the job.

- o Showing up at the academy with your boxer's pulled up and your blue jeans sagging like a gang banger.

- o Showing up for your first day wearing an "*I love the ACLU*" button.

- Wearing a Hemp T-shirt under your uniform.

- Showing off multiple piercings of your tongue, neck, and lips.

- Texting or listening to an IPod during your first day of academy class.

- **What the driver said:** *"This won't hurt my chances, will it?"*

- **What the officer heard:** *"I'm drunk and in denial. I will need the next two years to get my life together. Go ahead and pull my name from consideration for hiring."*

EXCUSE NUMBER 74

When stopped after going 85 MPH for six miles with a State Trooper on his tail with flashing lights the driver stated,

"Where the hell were you hiding?"

Risk Rating: High Risk - One Donut

Your Excuse Sucks & You're at Risk

Hiding? Where the hell was I hiding? Shake the dumb bugs out of your noggin, son! The cop was behind you for six miles. That's enough time to eat lunch, sip on a cup of coffee, and indulge in an extra doughnut or two. In fact, this was a three donut excuse at the start of the pursuit. The officer ate two of the donuts during the chase and now it is only a one donut excuse. Next time, pull over numb nuts!

What a silly question to ask! Most career speeders have this thought on the tip of their tongues when they notice the red and blue flashing lights in the rearview mirror. But this driver came out and said it after six miles of pursuit! Thus, I have a certain amount of respect for this honest yet blatant offender.

So, he only get's one donut and that's because he said something honest and because the other two donuts were consumed during the chase.

- **What the driver said:** *"Where the hell were you hiding?"*

- **What the officer heard:** *"I had my head up my ass because I'm comfortable speeding. I speed all the time. Five years ago I was a career speed demon and kept a close eye on the rear view mirror. Then I rear ended a guy who had stopped in front of me and I got a ticket for that.*

  So, now I watch out for cars in front of me and you sneaky bastards pull this little trick. You snuck up behind me, in broad daylight, with a fully marked police car. That's not fair. I pay taxes and expect MORE than this. Write me MORE tickets."

EXCUSE NUMBER 75

When stopped for speeding on a dark, rainy night,
the driver claimed,

"We're just trying to get home and out of the rain."

Risk Rating: Moderate Risk - Three Donuts

A So-So Excuse to Use on 5-0

This excuse is dangerously charming and almost makes sense, inspiring the officer to listen and look carefully. *"Hmm, going home and out of the rain?* Well, the car is driving southbound and according to the license, the home is northbound. This driver is not going home and just told a big fat fib. Does this cap rationale sound petty, minor, and unfair? It's not!

If a driver is willing to lie during a minor traffic stop, he's unwilling to change his bad habits. This excuse earned a $400 ticket for negligent driving. **Don't lie.** Instead of lying, consider purchasing one of those oversized beach umbrellas and holding it over your car when it rains. Now, that would be charming.

- **What the driver said:** *"We're just trying to get home and out of the rain."*

- **What the officer heard:** *"I lie about my golf score, my waist size, and I'm willing to lie about* *a minor traffic violation. I'm the kind of guy that takes off his wedding ring on business trips. Lying is just part of my DNA. Officer, this may be your only chance to nudge me toward becoming more honest. May the tickets rain down on me!"*

EXCUSE NUMBER 76

When stopped for suspicion of drunk driving (with a resulting blood alcohol of .22), the driver, a Children's Ballet Instructor, claimed,

"Officer, I'm on my way to work. I can't be drunk."

Risk Rating: No Donut - Prance from the car!

You Probably Blew It! Good Luck!

I'll let you in on a police secret: If you have a job that impacts the elderly or children, we will look closely at you and your habits. We will scrutinize you as a role model more closely than an ultimate cage fighter, home builder, adult film maker or snake charmer. Any hint of drug or alcohol involvement will lead to quick and stern enforcement.

- **What the driver said:** *"Officer, I'm on my way to work. I can't be drunk."*

- **What the officer heard:** *"Officer, I'm on my way to getting drunk. I can't be at work. Many of the parents know about my malady already; however, I work with the upper crust of society's bread and they don't want to say anything. Could you do me a favor? Please arrest me and prominently post my name in the daily* *news. This will really help me out and the parents will love you for it."*

- **Final thought:** *Driver - AKA: Ballet Instructor - had a .22 Blood Alcohol Count upon arrest. No wonder she can do the splits!*

  Come to think of it, that's the only time I've been able to do the splits. I used to get hurt every time I drank. My friends could always predict when I would be going to the Emergency Room for some stitches or treatment. They knew they should call the ambulance every time they heard me say, **"Watch this."**

EXCUSE NUMBER 77

*After being stopped for running several stop signs,
the driver stated,*

"Officer, I really stepped in it … didn't I?"

Risk Rating: Moderate Risk - Three Donuts

A So-So Excuse to Use on 5-0

I know, I know: You're thinking this is going to be another poop joke or something along those lines. Nope! Sorry! It's not. This justification was an expression of speech made by a teen that knew when he'd been caught doing something wrong. He was in what we call the *"surrender ritual."* *"I'm done"* … no fight, no argument, no smack talking!

Officers are fond of earnestness and acceptance used by those we stop, so this young man's justification merited a *"moderate"* three donut risk rating. Suggestion: you should note your prototype within the lucrative excuses. Suggestion two: Look at some of your past favorites within these pages and decide on the type or theme that works for you – something within the last seventy-five excuses that feels comfortable to you.

- **What the driver said:** *"Officer, I really stepped in it … didn't I?"*

- **What the officer heard:** *"Officer, I messed up. While I hoped it wouldn't come to this, you caught me by surprise. I am willing to change and willing to take my medicine without any honey. In confessing, I'm making it very easy for you to write a ticket that will not be challenged in court. I'm equally surprised you're giving me a stern warning and no ticket. Whew!"*

- **Final thought:** *While risky, falling on your sword often works.*

EXCUSE NUMBER 78

During sobriety testing on an 81 year old male suspected of driving while intoxicated, the officer asked him if he had anything that may interfere with the physical sobriety tests. He answered,

"Physical stuff? Oh, yea. I'm wearing some heavy duty diapers."

Risk Rating: Moderate Risk - Three Donuts

A So-So Excuse to Use on 5-0

Whoa! This surprised officer expected something like, *"Yep, I've got a knee replacement ... a glass eye or I've got a stiff neck or back."* Never before had the officer heard "I may lose control of my bowels and therefore I'm wearing a king sized diaper." So the officer smiled and this excuse earned a "moderate" rating.

It's interesting how people interpret the question about "physical defects" differently. The question is usually stated like, "Before sobriety tests, do you have any physical defects, pain, or injuries I should know about?" Some classic responses include:

- *"Officer, you are pain in my butt right now."*

- *"Shoot yeah, I'm drunk as heck."*

- *"I have some hair on my chin (female)."*

- *"I think this is going to hurt my pocket book."*

- *"If I wasn't loaded, I'd probably have a panic attack."*

- **What the driver said:** *"Physical stuff? Oh yea. I'm wearing some heavy duty diapers."*

- **What the officer heard:** *"Officer, I'm old, very honest and a little tipsy. I likely fought in one of the World Wars. I'm not a bad guy – I'm just having a little trouble in my older years. While I will accept an arrest honorably, I appreciate any leniency you may offer."*

- **Final thought:** *This man was taken home without arrest or citation. Hmm, the truth seems to be working quite well.*

EXCUSE NUMBER 79

When paced from behind by an officer, 86 in a 60 MPH zone, the driver stated,

"If I get a ticket, then YOU get one for driving just as fast as me."

Risk Rating: High Risk - One Donut

Your Excuse Sucks & You're at Risk

Oh, that's good … Oh, my sides … You're killing me … Stop! There's that rationale again! If you use this declaration, probability is high you are getting a ticket. This is humorous and one we don't hear regularly. So, the risk rating depends on the way it's delivered – voice intonation, timing, and facial demonstration. This driver flunked on timing (and more) as it was the first thing he said to the officer. Poor form, poor delivery, poor pocket book, and poor insurance rates for the next five years. $Cha-ching$!

- **What the driver said:** *"If I get a ticket, then YOU get one for driving just as fast as me."*

- **What the officer heard:** *"I'm so excited officer! I've been practicing this line and hoping some day to use it. How did I do? What do you mean 'Your excuse sucks and you're at risk?' I've tried this out in the mirror and he liked it, with my lying friends at the tavern and they loved it, and in front of my fearful family. They all said it was a dandy excuse and I should use* *it as soon as possible. My friends and family, who are all sick of me, said I should preface it with the F-word; however, I didn't add that. What the hell do you mean by that …*

'No Donut – Step out of the car?'

Officer, I'm not sure what that means. OUCH! Okay, I'm getting it."

EXCUSE NUMBER 80

When stopped for speeding 50 in a 35 MPH zone in a car - with five lawyers yelling at each other - and one angry driver (telling the lawyers to "shut up"), the driver stated,

"Officer, I'm trying to get back to the office and away from these guys (thumbing toward the back seat)!"

Risk Rating: Yes! Five Donuts! - Low Risk!

A Fantastic Excuse to Use on *THE MAN*

The aggrieved pain on the driver's face, the legal background noise, the smell of nice suits soaked in sweat, the Volvo Station wagon in complete pandemonium, the crumpled legal papers all over the car, and the angry comment made by the driver, all added up to a "low" rating.

What good would a ticket serve? The Volvo is akin to a self-cleaning oven and the extremely high heat will cleanse the situation on its own.

- **What the driver said:** *"Officer, I'm trying to get back to the office and away from these guys (thumbing toward the back seat)!"*

- **What the officer heard:** *"Officer, I'm considering a career-change. Do you have an application for the police department? Yes,* *officer, we have something in common as I also have a disdain for defense lawyers. Officer, you probably heard the saying, 'it's sounds like a bunch of little old ladies?' I have to tell you, the saying should have been 'they sound like a bunch of little defense lawyers.' I don't care if you book my ass into jail … just help me!"*

EXCUSE NUMBER 81

*When a possible drunk driver was asked if he could
walk toe-to-toe on a white line,
the driver answered,*

"No, but I can step on YOUR toes."

**This comment was followed by the driver
stomping on the officer's foot and laughing.**

**Risk Rating: No Donut – Then hauled back
to the officer's car!**

**You definitely blew it! Heck with
good luck! Burn!**

Okay, because this is rated PG, I will not describe
exactly what the officer said or did; however, his car-
cam recorded the action.   Can you picture the
courtroom trial of this person: *"Your Honor, the driver
was too drunk to perform physical tests but, after
stomping on my foot, he gets a perfect score in how he
handled a justified police thumping."* By the way, that
little stomp on 5-0's foot led to a felony charge.

- **What the driver said:** *"No, but I can step on
  YOUR toes."*

- **What the officer heard:** *"Officer, I feel like I'm
  starring in an under arm deodorant commercial.
  First, you demonstrate the stick, then the spray,*

night stick, pepper spray, more spray, then the stick. I can't decide which you prefer. Oh, you're going to give me another sample? More stick ...ouch! Then more spray ... it stings my eyes!"

EXCUSE NUMBER 82

When stopped for speeding, 39 in a 25 MPH zone,
the driver stated,

"Come on man, don't you have anything better to do?"

Risk Rating: High Risk - One Donut

Your Excuse Sucks & You're at Risk

FISH ON! This guarantees at least one ticket for the original reason the driver was stopped. When a traffic cop hears a statement like this one, something very powerful happens to him or her inside. His or her powers of observation become extremely keen. More violations are noticed: No litterbag, a little weed in the ashtray, no seat belts, expired insurance, no proof of registration in the car, a slow oil leak considered an environmental hazard, and so on.

The original ticket seemed minor as the wave of several more crashed down on this driver...for whatever the officer could sniff out. To answer the driver's question, *"No, I don't have anything better to do right now. You just became my new hobby!"*

- **What the driver said:** *"Come on man, don't you have anything better to do?"*

- **What the officer heard:** *"Do you want me to lock my car before you book my ass into jail or will you handle that? Do I call my lawyer* *now or do we do it at the booking desk? Do we do the very special body search for drugs now or later? Later? Okay, I need to go to the bathroom really bad."*

- **Final thought:** *Are you noticing a pattern in the excuses that don't work?*

EXCUSE NUMBER 83

Late at night, this driver in a high end sports car was stopped for speeding (in excess of 90 in a 60 MPH zone. The professional athlete stated,

"No way man, I wasn't even out of third gear."

Risk Rating: Moderate Risk - Three Donuts

A So-So Excuse to Use on 5-0

This is considered a high speed stop and would normally be a high-risk excuse to use. The statement is considered *Moderate Risk* for a number of reasons: First, it is honest. What this jock said seems to be plausible. Secondly, the officer understands the potential of the sports car and its speed. Finally, it's late at night and our basketball star has not been drinking and this is rare.

Most officers appreciate all three of these facts and understand the temptation to break loose on the open road. Unlike a previous lesson, this driver actually is a VIP who did not let his ego get the best of him.

- **What the driver said:** *"No way man, I wasn't even out of third gear."*

- **What the officer heard:** *"No way man, I respectfully disagree; however, I'm open to change. I will accept a ticket, officer, but greatly appreciate the warning."*

EXCUSE NUMBER 84

After stopped for following too close on the freeway at 65 MPH (about seven feet between the driver and the forward car), the driver stated,

"Officer, I wanted that bastard in front of me to see my eyes so he'd move out of the way!"

Risk Rating: High Risk - One Donut

Your Excuse Sucks & You're at Risk

Uh oh, **DUIR**; Driving Under the Influence of Rage! This driver is a tyrant! He is an asphalt terrorist trying to control others through aggressive driving, giving nasty glances and expressions to those who refuse to get out of his way. These are the drivers who wave as they drive - the one-finger wave. The only thing that lowered the risk rating on this event was his honesty.

Officers love to give these driver's a Load-O-Tickets. When we stop someone for this behavior we might be saving a life. If you run into one of these jerks, avoid eye contact and by all means, don't wave back. While we appreciate honesty, it didn't work in this case. Too little – too late!

- **What the driver said:** *"Officer, I wanted that bastard in front of me to see my eyes so he'd move out of the way!"*

- **What the officer heard:** *"I am a nasty control freak. I am the person who yells at the 16 year* *old McDonald's employee because the Big Mac took 90 seconds instead of 60. I am the goof who writes the local newspaper to complain about having to slow down in a school zone. I am the type of person who has no relationships or children because I use my personality for contraception. Yes, of course I need a ticket."*

- **Final thought:** *Remember, we love the smell and taste of sweet justice. Whenever an opportunity presents itself such as this one, we will mete out a little righteousness.*

EXCUSE NUMBER 85

When stopped for running a red light, the driver stated,

"Don't you have anything better to do?
There are real crooks out here!"

Risk Rating: High Risk - One Donut

Your Excuse Sucks & You're at Risk

What are we supposed to do with this? *"Oh, I'm sorry. You're absolutely right ... I'll let you go and get back on the beat - searching for the killers of the world. Go ... get out of here ... I'm really sorry for being so misled."* Under this kind of stress, some drivers try what's called a **Head Fake**. A head fake is the same trick used in sports (look one direction and throw the ball the other way).

This was also a ploy this officer experienced at his boyhood dinner table. The little-boy-now-officer's brother would steal food from his dinner plate. The delinquent sibling would say, *"Hey look, the Goodyear Blimp"* - pointing out the window followed by the theft of food while officer-as-a-boy was distracted. It worked when the officer was nine years old, but it doesn't work anymore.

This driver tried the head fake, blurted out something stupid, and was also a wee bit too nervous. A computer check produced an arrest warrant for a bucket load of lawless stuff. Also, please remember that **Don't-you-have-anything-better-to-do** is seven words that bring out the wrath-of-cop.

- **What the driver said:** *"Don't you have anything better to do? There are real crooks out here!"*

- **What the officer heard:** *"Hey look, the Goodyear Blimp."*

- **Final thought:** *Let the officer set the tone of the traffic stop. If he's a jerk, you may dare to adjust. Start nice and hopefully stay nice!*

EXCUSE NUMBER 86

A drunk driver drove his pickup around the warning gate and through a military checkpoint.
He told the officers,

"Hey, I pay taxes and might as well own this Army Post."

Risk Rating: Step into MY Patrol car!

You Undoubtedly Blew It! Good Luck!

Yeah right, brilliance! An unavoidable and distressing pattern of drunk drivers is that they have no responsibility and actually believe their own B.S. The evidence is so clear in this situation that a jury made up of Al Qaeda would convict this guy for blowing the gate. Did you notice the driver still had to make up a conceivable excuse? One might think if you're drunk driving you may want to avoid a military checkpoint. Yes, this guy didn't even live on the military base. Ouch!

- **What the driver said:** *"Hey, I pay taxes and might as well own this army post."*

- **What the officer heard:** *"Hey, I used to be a lawyer in my fantasy. I'm a clear thinking constitutionalist – when I'm sober."*

EXCUSE NUMBER 87

When stopped for speeding, the driver claimed,

"Three guys are chasing me."

Risk Rating: Moderate Risk - Three Donuts

A So-So Excuse to Use on 5-0

Running from others is a bad sign! It is not common and will only work if you can produce the "Three Guys." Not so great when the officer can't find the three guys or whatever you're running from. You can easily bump this excuse into the "High Risk - One Donut" category if you don't provide a name or a reason you are being chased.

You can also create a real problem for yourself if you say *"Some black guys are chasing me."* That one is truly overused and not very nice. In any case, if those "guys" are on your tail, look at your lifestyle or move out of our jurisdiction.

- **What the driver said:** *"Three guys are chasing me."*

- **What the officer heard:** *"Officer, I said 'Three' because it is the number I always use when I'm lying. 'Guys are chasing me' is the term I use every time I'm looking around to score some dope and I run into you! I'm just avoiding responsibility for my actions.*

Hmmm… you can't call me a liar so just write me a ticket instead."

- **Final thought:** *If someone is chasing you, drive to a fire station or a police department. Don't make the mistake this guy made and keep driving circles in the area known for street level narcotic sales.*

EXCUSE NUMBER 88

When stopped and questioned because of suspected drunk driving, the driver told the officer,

"Save the lecture police girl.
Just take me to jail."

Risk Rating: You know!

Here's what happened after this driver's statement:

Officer: "Excuse me?"

Driver: "You deaf? I said I don't want any of your sh*!. Just take me to jail."

Officer: "Gladly. Step out of the car!"

Driver: "No!"

Officer: "I am so glad you said '*NO*.'"

Not too smart, Home Slice! Slam the officer and make a biased comment about her gender. I'll spare you the gruesome details; however, be sufficient to say, a human can exit an automobile window…with a little help and some assistance from Police Girl.

- **What the driver said:** *"Save the lecture police girl. Just take me to jail."*

- **What the officer heard:** *"Go police girl, go! Taze me until I pee in my skinny designer jeans all the way down to my low-cut Converse. Is that all you got girly-girl? Come on, I said TAZE me. Give me every volt and amp you've got! That a girl. Now we're communicating."*

- **Final thought:** *Never, and I mean NEVER underestimate the physical power of an officer. Female, male, short, fat as they have tools on a tool belt and know how to use everyone of them. If the tools won't suffice, they pick up that little portable radio and ask for back up.*

EXCUSE NUMBER 89

*When stopped for suspicion of drunk driving,
the driver claimed,*

"I couldn't be drunk, Officer. I'm on my way to the bar."

Risk Rating: High Risk - One Donut

Your Excuse Sucks & You're at Risk

Back in my drinking days, it was considered normal to pre-lube up with a couple of stiff drinks before I went to the bar. It was a matter of economics; throw some good, strong stuff in the gut and nurse one or two expensive drinks at the bar.

Such was the case with this woman, except she had a little more than a couple of pre-drinks. She put the officer in a precarious position; should he go ahead and let her go to a bar to continue drinking, perhaps hitting a busload of girl scouts on her way home? No way.

As I said, it turned out her pre-drinking involved more than a couple of drinks. She blew a .19 on the Breathalyzer – well over the legal limit. At this alcohol level, she was in the condition of a drunk heading home after a night on the town!

- **What the driver said:** *"I couldn't be drunk, Officer. I'm on my way to the bar."*

- **What the officer heard:** *"I'm buzzed already and behind the wheel … and going to be in a business that primarily serves more booze. I don't know just how much trouble my little alcoholic body is in. Can you help me?"*

EXCUSE NUMBER 90

When stopped for crossing the center line and nearly sideswiping an oncoming police car, the driver claimed,

"Something flew up my dress and bit me."

Risk Rating: Yes! Five Donuts! - Low Risk!

A Fantastic Excuse to Use on *THE MAN*

How does an officer disprove this excuse? "*Well, Miss; I'm going to need to see that sting before I'll let you off.*" Yeah, right! Stung or not, this is a brilliant excuse to use. But remember, the driver's "*bee boogie*" looks a lot like a grand mal seizure. An officer is just as sharp as a bee's stinger and will look for some evidence of this dance.

Did you frantically gyrate as you came across the center line? Were the car's windows open? Is it even the season for bugs that bite? Is there a dead bee on your floorboard? Are you scratching your … um, your bite while talking with the officer?

Police drive thousand of miles each year, many times with their windows open. They know the bee boogie firsthand. The biting bug is a great excuse…if it's true.

- **What the driver said:** *"Something flew up my dress and bit me.*

- **What the officer heard**: *"I'm sober and having a tough day. I would never consider crossing the center line into the path of a police car. Something horrible was unfolding in my car and I panicked. What good would a ticket serve?"*

- **Final thought:** *A driver is in great shape when the evidence supports your verbal excuse provided.*

EXCUSE NUMBER 91

A car was chased for over two miles though alleyways and around street corners by a patrol car showing lights and sirens. When the officer walked up to the window, the driver asked,

"Did you want me or someone else?"

Risk Rating: Let me help you out of the car, at gunpoint!

You definitely blew it! Good Luck!

Give me a break! *"No sir, it's just a coincidence that you happened to be in front of my patrol car on a high-speed chase where we took the same fourteen turns, cut across five of the same parking lots, two alleyways, and the three identical U-turns. It's also a miracle that we happened to park in the same spot on the same shoulder. It is NO coincidence that my gun is out and pointed at YOU."* Truly a dangerous juvenile attempt and excuse!

In fact, after this type of pursuit you will be taken out of your car very carefully and under the watchful eyes of more than one officer. This will get you booked and your car searched! This kind of disregard for an emergency vehicle really burns our butts and is normally a felony.

- **What the driver said:** *"Did you want me or someone else?"*

- **What the officer heard:** *"I'm dangerous, I'm wild, I'm unpredictable, and you should use great caution when you approach me. Please search me and my car. You will likely find additional evidence in support of my wild-assed driving.*

- **Final thought:** *Yes, drugs were located in the car. Surprise, surprise.*

EXCUSE NUMBER 92

When stopped for several traffic violations,
the driver stated,

"Hey Cop, last time I checked – you
work for me."

Risk Rating: High Risk - One Donut

Your Excuse Sucks & You're at Risk

Okay, let me try to explain how this little fit of dysfunction goes over with 5-0. Just because officers are paid out of the tax base, John Q. Citizen feels it necessary to tell us this. Again, the truth is not the issue – timing is the issue. Deciding to use political or constitutional activism in the middle of a traffic stop never works. NEVER WORKS! Did you hear me? Not *sometimes* doesn't work, *occasionally* may work, if the *cop's in a good mood it might work.* **IT NEVER WORKS!** So, knock it off!

It's hard for officers to swallow assertive or headstrong contentions from the average citizen, political activist, or even the mayor. To set the record straight, we do have a boss. His name is GOD. Put that in your little whiney pipe and smoke it, if you dare!

- **What the driver said:** *"Hey Cop, last time I checked - you work for me."*

- **What the officer heard:** *"Hey officer, I should be on mood stabilizing medication. Yes, this is me at my best. I also believe that my wife works for me, my boss works for me, and the world works for me. Interestingly enough, what hasn't been working for me since childhood is my attitude.*

   You just don't know how hard it is, walking through life with an absolute sense of entitlement. It is difficult being right all the time and I need help with my humility ... whatever the hell that word means. Oh, thank you! Four tickets should help."

EXCUSE NUMBER 93

When a suspected drunk driver pulled into a private driveway and ran over a garbage can and a Big Wheel Tricycle, his story:

"Well, Ossifer, it's my son's deal to keep the driveway clear every Friday night."

Risk Rating: No Donut - Step out of the car!

You COMPLETELY Blew It! Bye-Bye!

Clear the driveway *"Every Friday night?"* Your son's responsibility is to clear the driveway before you come home drunk? This kind of puts the entire family into the *"bad day"* experience. This is horrible and the officer's actions will reflect it. The officers investigating this accident gathered all the evidence, took a statement from the son, and took the drunk's statement, which they labeled a *"drunk-o-log."* This driver is what we call a *conditioned drunk* in the mid to late stages of alcoholism. The worst part, he now involves his children in covering his pickled ass … watching out for him while in his polluted condition. I still get angry as I write this one!

- **What the driver said:** *"Well, Ossifer, it's my son's deal to keep the driveway clear every Friday night."*

- **What the officer heard:** *"Officer, in order to save my family and any shred of hope they have, throw the book at me. Yes, book me and charge me with everything you can; DUI, Reckless Driving, Endangering a Child, and go ahead and write me for not covering my mouth when I sneeze."*

- **Final thought:** *By the way, the driver had pulled into the wrong driveway. Yep, the neighbor's driveway, two doors down. His son, as ordered, had cleared his driveway earlier in the afternoon.*

EXCUSE NUMBER 94

*When stopped for multiple traffic violations,
the driver stated,*

"What's up, policeman? That's how I drive."

Risk Rating: High Risk - One Donut

Your Excuse Sucks & You're at Risk

Oh boy! This is a tad bit of a problem. Talk about an incriminating statement. Ouch! Do not try this one as it does not work with the officer, the courts, or with the Department of Licensing. With your fourth wife? Maybe. But not with *The Man*!

What in the world was the driver expecting to hear, *"Okay, no problem Mr. Driver. Feel free to continue DWHUA – Driving with Head Up Ass."* Oooo, it's really dark, and awkward, and strange up here. Can someone please turn on a light?

Too Funny! We have no option but to scratch out a ticket when the attitude is not self-correcting. Think about what I just said,

WE HAVE ABSOLUTELY NO OPTION BUT TO TAKE ENFORCEMENT ACTION WHEN THE ATTITUDE IS NOT SELF-CORRECTING.

- **What the driver said:** *"What's up, policeman? That's how I drive."*

- **What the officer heard:** *"But Officer, I drive like a jerk all the time. I've done a whole bunch of jerky driving that you blind police haven't caught me doing. Officer, I need a whole bunch of those tickets because I don't plan on stopping my jerky driving. Why you say? Because I'm never wrong!"*

EXCUSE NUMBER 95

When stopped for speeding (clocked on radar going 65 in a 45 MPH zone), the driver stated,

"Officer, I just love you guys. I watch Forensic Files ... and COPS ... and that Bounty Dog guy ... and Repo Man."

Risk Rating: Moderate Risk - Three Donuts

A So-So Excuse to Use on 5-0

The mantra of some traffic violators is: ***In a rut? Try sucking up!*** Do you know what? It usually works! Regardless of what our police officers claim in public, they love it. Yes, it depends on the officer's mood and the seriousness of the offense. If you have no other excuses that come to mind, tell police officers how great they look or how professional they are. Ask us about our career goals, dangers of the job, and how we handle all the stress. It might just work.

- **What the driver said:** *"Officer, I just love you guys. I watch Forensic Files ... and COPS ... and that Bounty Dog guy ... and Repo Man."*

- **What the officer heard:** *"I'm a groupie and I'm really over doing it. I may be infatuated with you or I might just be a total situational suck up. I may only love you right at the moment; however, I may REALLY love everything about you. As for the future of our relationship, it's* *your call. If I need a ticket – so be it! I will cherish the little pink or golden paper bearing your name. MY policeman! Mmmm, mmmm, good. Grrrr, growl, ruff"*

- **Final thought:** *Skip the part and avoid, "Mmmm, mmmm, good." Total overkill. Also, remember the context. If the officer is a total porker, skip it and move on to another smoke screen. He knows it. Don't screw yourself through an obvious lie.*

EXCUSE NUMBER 96

When stopped for speeding and lane travel, she said

"Officer, is it the bullet proof vest or just too much eating?"

Risk Rating: High Risk - One Donut

Your Excuse Sucks & You're at Risk

Why the "*high rating*?" Simple as this is the opposite of the standard *suck up* and will create some friction. The officer was in fact dieting and was a tad sensitive about his condition. Besides, the guys on a diet and a three donut warning would have been unhealthy for him.

Now, let's discuss the tone this young lady set for the next ten to fifteen minutes of her life. She's come to the party with two violations against her and she stomped on the officer's fragile ego via a FAT comment. This is not exactly the best way to start a short-term relationship. The traffic stop is now going to take thirty-five minutes or more, not because the officer wrote so many tickets, but because he is now preoccupied with himself, his gut, and his anger. The poor officer lost track of time as he texted a couple friends, his counselor, and researched the traffic laws to find four new violations that he hardly ever writes.

- **What the driver said:** *"Officer, is it the bullet proof vest or just too much eating?"*

- **What the officer heard:** *"Officer, I'm a cross between your over-bearing mother, the ex wife, and your personal doctor. No, I don't have the right to comment on the condition of your body; however, I'm a real bitch and do it habitually to others. I think the great equalizer would be a serious blow to my driving record. Go ahead and write away, butter buns ... I earned it."*

- **Final thought:** *As my mom said, "If you don't have anything nice to say ... EAT SOME SOAP!"*

EXCUSE NUMBER 97

When stopped for speeding and possible drunk driving,
the driver stated,

*"Hey Dragnet, I know what you're going to ask:
'Have you been drinking, how much, and
where did you have your last drink?' I'll make
it easy for you:*

*Yes, too much, and none of your F*ing
business."*

**Risk Rating: Once I get done laughing, No
Donut - Step out of the car! Actually, let me
drag your ass out of the car!**

You Blew It Beautifully! Off to Treatment!

Wow! You have to appreciate a drunk-o-log that is so
succinct, to the point, and absolutely condemning. You
should have smelled this excuse, whoa! It was a
combination of bad chili, stale whiskey, and dirty socks.
In a few years the technology will allow me to pump the
stench into your nostrils via this book.

The sensory experience with this pickle was over
powering, one that stayed in the officer's nose for a day
or two. The officer said *"I could actually taste the
smell."* Many times, we're shocked that such an
impaired mind can actually operate a motor vehicle and

communicate in such a direct and dysfunctional fashion!

- **What the driver said**: *"Hey Dragnet, I know what you're going to ask: 'Have you been drinking, how much, and where did you have your last drink?' I'll make it easy for you: Yes, too much, and none of your F*ing business."*

- **What the officer heard**: *"I'm so drunk I need my stomach pumped and one of those deep cleansing herbal enemas. I'm NEVER this honest when I'm on the water wagon."*

- **Final thought**: *.30 blood alcohol count. Yowee! He was taken to the hospital and then to detox and jail. No trial. Surprise, surprise … He pleaded guilty.*

EXCUSE NUMBER 98

A driver was placed under arrest when stopped for running a stop sign and found to have a revoked driver's license because of unpaid traffic tickets. The driver stated,

"Does it help if I have a license under another name and date of birth?"

Risk Rating: No Donut - Step out of the car!

You Probably Blew It ... plus some!
Good Luck!

Remember when I explained what happens when you are really honest with the officer? This is not the type of honesty I was talking about. This is called "Tombstone Honesty." It's truthful, but someone is going to lose big time. This excuse adds more fuel to an already out-of-control wildfire.

Now the officer has about seven charges to pick from. It's not fair giving the officer that may choices. It's stressful, akin to trying to pick the cutest puppy out of a litter of seven delightful and loveable doggies. They are all so beautiful, so meaningful, so perfect. Can I take all of them? Yep! In this case the officer also took advantage of all seven charges.

- **What the driver said:** *"Does it help if I have a license under another name and date of birth?*

- **What the officer heard:** *"Does it help if I put my hands behind my back now? How about I just handcuff myself? Do you prefer to search the car for my stolen checks and credit cards or can I just tell you where they are?"*

EXCUSE NUMBER 99

When stopped for weaving from lane to land, no headlights on (at 1:00 A.M.), and suspected intoxication, the driver stated,

"Officer, this is getting old. Why are YOU screwing with me all the time?"

Risk Rating: High Risk - One Donut

Your Excuse Sucks & You're at Risk

Let's see ... "*Getting old*" followed by "*YOU*" followed by "*All the time.*"   To quote a famous astronaut, *Houston, we have a pattern*. The driver could have had better results by saying, "*I didn't do it this time. Yes, all the other times ... just not this time.*" Due to the driver's suicidal words, the officer thinks he's got a live one. This guy is armed with excuses and quick to blame. The Police Shrink calls this dirty little habit **transference**; moving attention away from the one at fault and onto another target.

At this point, the officer needs to recall the violations and stay focused; "*headlights off, cannot stay in his own lane of travel, smells like a keg of bad beer, and wants to point the finger at me.*" Poor form, superstar. The sum total puts the driver into what the Army refers to as a "*target-rich environment.*"   An arrest is inevitable and he'll be sure to hit the intended target!

- **What the driver said:** *"Officer, this is getting old. Why are YOU screwing with me all the time?"*

- **What the officer heard:** *"Officer, I was never spanked as a child and have always been able to slink my way out of trouble. My communication strategy works very well with my alcoholic girlfriend. Why doesn't it work on you?"*

- **Final thought:** *How close is this statement to humor, accountability, and responsibility? Right! Not even close. Pick the form and substance of an excuse that works for you … while containing all the right elements.*

EXCUSE NUMBER 100

When stopped for driving 50 in a 30 MPH zone and for running several stop signs/red lights, the driver was found hunched over the driver's seat, crying,

"Oh please, I got a hell of a hernia goin' mon!"

Risk Rating: Yes! Five Donuts! - Low Risk!

A Fantastic Excuse to Use on *THE MAN*

This visitor from Jamaica was in trouble and to make matters worse, he was on vacation and suffering horribly! An honest driver on vacation, in pain, lost and trying to find a hospital adds up to *"Five Donuts! & Low Risk*!." Any officer who'd write a ticket to someone in this predicament should see the Police Shrink.

Have you ever had a bursting hernia? Oh MON, it's like havin' a co-co nut in dee tube. Oh Mon, very painful.

- **What the driver said:** *"Oh please, I got a hell of a hernia goin' mon!"*

- **What the officer heard:** *"Officer, I'm not faking it. In addition to my authentic words, I'm sober, have labored breathing, and have little sweat beads forming on my forehead and neck. While it's probably my Appendix preparing for exit and not a hernia, that's the only thing I could say with my poor grasp of English."*

- **Final thought:** *The officer in this case escorted the guy to the hospital and then confirmed the malady. Appendicitis! O' mon! Tank you, my bruddah!*

EXCUSE NUMBER 101

A young college student was stopped for speeding (74 in a 60 MPH zone) and it was found that while she had a valid driver's license, she did not have a driver's license in the state where she was stopped, the state where she was attending college, or the state where she lives with her parents. She explained,

"To be honest, I get my driver's license in the least expensive state!"

Risk Rating: Moderate Risk - Three Donuts

A So-So Excuse to Use on 5-0

You'd be surprised how often we run into this little dilemma. It happens in relation to both the expense of a driver's license and trying to find the cheapest license plates and tabs. While we understand the joy in searching for a coupon special, all the related traffic violations are expensive.

The risk rating is based on three things: The officer's mood at the time, seriousness of the traffic violation, and the driver's attitude and delivery. While not the case here, a serious traffic violation will cook your goose every time.

- **What the driver said:** *"To be honest, I get my driver's license in the least expensive state!"*

- **What the officer heard:** "I'm *honest, courteous, and I'm trying to get through college. While looking for the best deal, I offer no threat to anyone and I'm trying to live right.*"

- **Final thought:** *This driver received what we call a "fix it" ticket. If the driver amends the error before court, all charges are dropped.*

EXCUSE NUMBER 102

An elderly pastor, in full garb, was stopped for speeding and no left tail light. After the officer explained the violations, the man responded,

"We missed you in church last Sunday, is everything going okay?"

Risk Rating: No Risk

A Fantastic Excuse to Use on *THE MAN*

The officer answered, "*Pastor John, I didn't recognize you.*" Yes, even the men and women of the cloth commit driving errors. My pastor is always a little over the speed limit as he rushes to some birth, or funeral, or bingo match. Do we write up our own pastors? Absolutely not! After all, some things are sacred.

- **What the driver said:** *"We missed you in church last Sunday, is everything going okay?"*

- **What the officer heard:** *"Don't even think about writing a ticket."*

ABOUT THE AUTHOR

Marcus (Mark) Mann is a former police officer and chief who worked in a myriad of Law Enforcement roles in Washington State for over 20 years. He is a former K9 handler, Team Leader for the Hostage Negotiations Team, A Critical Incident Stress Counselor, and was the Program Supervisor for Washington's Police Academy Training. He's written and produced books and videos on a variety of police, risk management, and public safety topics. This is his third book and first best seller (wishful thinking). He's currently working on his fourth book, ***Kiln-Fired Change; When Change is No Longer Optional.***

Marcus is the Owner and Principal of Sound Predictions, a premier consultation, training, and coaching company, which he founded and considers his fulltime vocation (www.SoundPredictions.com). In addition to coaching and performance counseling, he provides high energy and humorous keynote and training presentations internationally.

Marcus has worked a successful training, speaking, and comical platform throughout the United States and internationally in Bogota (2009), Montreal (2008), Germany, London (2002), Medellin (2009), Regina, Saskatchewan, and other countries. Regardless of his love for travel, he cherishes his home in the beautiful Puget Sound region of Washington State and considers his second home to be Kona, Hawaii. Marcus balances his program through hiking, gardening, and running with his two dogs.

If interested in training services or the hilarious Keynote Presentation, ***No Quota,*** you may contact Marcus directly through the email link at his website:

www.SoundPredictions.com

Final thought from the author:

I sincerely hope you enjoyed this book and I greatly appreciate your purchase and time in reading it. While we laughed at some of the antics outlined in these pages, the destructive results of poor driving and DUI are not so funny.

This purchase and all future sales of **No Quota** will be used wisely; dedicated to the victims, young and old, forever impacted by the reckless disregard of drunken drivers. Also, a percentage of the proceeds generated through book sales will be intelligently directed toward the untreated alcoholic and addict as we leverage them toward finding the real solution.

Bottom Line: A portion of the money generated by this publication will go directly to nonprofit victim and treatment outreach services.

Please drive carefully, drive dry, and keep your bloodstream and head clear. Through doing this, you may wisely consider and crank out the best excuse when stopped by *The Man!*

Thank you and God bless,

Marcus Mann, Principal

www.SoundPredictions.com

Made in the USA
Charleston, SC
06 February 2010